WITHDRAWN

PAKISTAN

From 1947 to the Creation of Bangladesh

KEESING'S RESEARCH REPORT

PAKISTAN

From 1947 to the Creation of Bangladesh

CHARLES SCRIBNER'S SONS

New York

DS
384
P325

The maps on pages 53 and 122 are reprinted with the permission of *The Economist*.

The map on page 112 is reprinted with the permission of *The Times*, London. Copyright © 1971.

Copyright © 1973 Keesing's Publications (Longman Group Ltd.)

This book published simultaneously in the
United States of America and in Canada—
Copyright under the Berne Convention

All rights reserved. No part of this book
may be reproduced in any form without the
permission of Charles Scribner's Sons.

1 3 5 7 9 11 13 15 17 19 C/C 20 18 16 14 12 10 8 6 4 2
1 3 5 7 9 11 12 15 17 19 C/P 20 18 16 14 12 10 8 6 4 2

Printed in the United States of America
Library of Congress Catalog Card Number 73-2553
SBN 684-13407-1 (cloth)
SBN 684-13408-X (paper)

CONTENTS

I. THE ESTABLISHMENT OF PAKISTAN   1
The Transfer of Power—The Indian Independence Act—Area and Population of Pakistan in 1948—Accession of Separate States—Mass Movement of Population following Partition of the Punjab—The "Pathanistan" Issue—Inaugural Meeting of the Constituent Assembly—Karachi proclaimed Capital—Death of Mr. Jinnah

II. EFFORTS AT FORMULATION OF A CONSTITUTION, 1949–1954   17
Preparatory Work on the Constitution—The Objectives Resolution—First and Second Reports of Basic Principles Committee—Directive Principles of State Policy—Fundamental Rights Committee—Representation in Federal Legislature—Amendments to the Constitution—Political Developments during 1953—Dissolution of Constituent Assembly—Declaration of State of Emergency—Provincial Developments, 1951–1954

III. MINORITY PROBLEMS AND BORDER
     DISPUTES, 1948–1959   37
     Talks on Minorities, 1948—Further Agreement on Minorities, April 1950—Karachi Talks on Indo-Pakistani Differences—Hindu Minorities in Pakistan—Increased Migration between India and Pakistan—Boundary Disputes—Border Incidents

IV. THE KASHMIR AND CANAL WATERS DISPUTES   45
    The Kashmir Problem—The Canal Waters Dispute—The Indus Waters Treaty

V. THE CONSTITUTION OF 1956—POLITICAL
    DEVELOPMENTS, 1956–1957—ABROGATION
    OF CONSTITUTION, 1958   59
    Election of New Constituent Assembly—The Constitution of the Islamic Republic of Pakistan—The Unified Province of West Pakistan—The Electorate Bill—Political Developments in Pakistan, 1956–1957—Cabinet Crisis and Abrogation of Constitution

VI. CONSTITUTIONAL DEVELOPMENTS UNDER
    AYUB KHAN, 1959–1962   76
    The Basic Democracies System—The New Constitution of 1962—Revival of Political Parties—Presidential Elections—National and Provincial Assembly Elections

VII. INDO-PAKISTANI RELATIONS, 1959–1966   86
     Communal Disturbances—Indo-Pakistani Hostilities in Rann of Kutch, 1965—The Kashmir Crisis of 1965—The Tashkent Declaration

VIII. THE BREAKDOWN OF PRESIDENT AYUB
      KHAN'S REGIME, 1969   94
      Student Protests and Mr. Bhutto's Agitation in West Pakistan—Agitation for Autonomy in East Pakistan—Growing Disorder in Both Wings—Ayub Khan's Resignation—Constitutional Developments

IX. PAKISTAN'S EAST WING BECOMES
     INDEPENDENT BANGLADESH   104
     The General Elections of 1970—The Build-up to Civil
     War in East Pakistan, December 1970–March 1971—
     The Outbreak of Civil War—Deterioration of Relations
     between India and Pakistan following Civil War—The
     Indo-Pakistan War—Bangladesh Government Estab-
     lished in Dacca—International Support for India and
     Pakistan—Moves towards Peace, 1972

APPENDIX I   128
     Pakistan's Alliances—South East Asia Treaty Organiza-
     tion (SEATO)—Central Treaty Organization (CENTO)
     —Regional Co-operation for Development (RCD)—
     Other Treaties

APPENDIX II   131
     Heads of State and of Government, 1947–1971

RECOMMENDED FURTHER READING   132

INDEX   135

ACKNOWLEDGMENTS

The following sources of information have been used in the compilation of this research report:

New York Times—International Herald Tribune—Times, London—*Daily Telegraph*, London—*The Guardian*, London—*Financial Times*, London—*Le Monde*, Paris—*Neue Zürcher Zeitung—Pakistan Times*, Lahore—*Dawn*, Karachi—*The Hindu*, Madras—*The Statesman*, Calcutta—*Peking Review*.

Foreign and Commonwealth Office, London—Soviet Embassy Press Department, London—U.S. Information Service—Pakistan High Commissioner's Office, London—Government Press Information Department, Rawalpindi—India High Commissioner's Office, London.

PAKISTAN

From 1947 to the
Creation of Bangladesh

I. THE ESTABLISHMENT OF PAKISTAN

THE TRANSFER OF POWER

At midnight on Aug. 14–15, 1947, the Indian Empire came to an end with the formal transfer of power by Britain to the two new Dominions of India and Pakistan, which came officially into existence.

The Pakistan Constituent Assembly met on Aug. 14 in special session at Karachi (Sind), the capital, to hear a message from Lord Mountbatten, the Viceroy. Lord Mountbatten first delivered a message to Pakistan and then addressed the Assembly as follows:

"I am speaking to you today as your Viceroy. Tomorrow the Government of Pakistan will rest in your hands, and I shall be the constitutional head of your neighbour, India. Tomorrow two new sovereign States will take their place in the Commonwealth. Not young nations, but the heirs of old and proud civilisations; independent States whose leaders and statesmen are known and respected throughout the world, whose poets and philosophers, scientists and warriors, have made their imperishable contribution to the service of mankind. Not immature Governments or weak, but fit to carry their great share of responsibility for the peace and progress of the world. The birth of Pakistan is an event in history.

". . . All this has been achieved with toil and sweat. I wish I could say also without tears and blood, but terrible crimes have been committed. It is justifiable to reflect, however, that far more terrible things might have happened if the majority had not proved worthy of the high endeavours of their leaders and had not listened to that great appeal which Mr. Jinnah and Mahatma Gandhi together made [see page 10].

"... This is a parting between friends who have learned to honour and respect one another even in disagreement. It is not an absolute parting, I rejoice to think, not an end of comradeship. Many of my countrymen for generations have been born in this country, many have lived their lives here and have died here. ... May Pakistan prosper always; may her citizens be blessed with health and happiness; may learning and the arts of peace flourish in her boundaries; and may she continue in friendship with her neighbours and with all the nations of the world."

Mr. Mohammed Ali Jinnah (who had earlier been invested with the title of *Quaid-i-Azam*, meaning "great leader") expressed the thanks and appreciation of Pakistan in a brief reply and said: "We are parting as friends, and I sincerely hope we shall remain friends."

On Aug. 15 Mr. Jinnah formally took the oath from Sir Abdur Rashid, Chief Justice of the Lahore High Court, as first Governor-General of Pakistan, after which he administered the oath of allegiance to Mr. Liaquat Ali Khan, Prime Minister of Pakistan, and the other members of the Pakistan Cabinet. The ceremony, which took place at Government House, commenced with the reading of a verse from the Koran, a 31-gun salute being fired as the *Quaid-i-Azam* assumed office and the Pakistani flag being hoisted.

The conception of a separate State for the Moslems of India, though at first regarded as visionary and impractical, had been put forward by Mr. Jinnah for several years and had won increasing support from Moslem opinion. In 1940 the Moslem League adopted the "Pakistan resolution", put forward by Mr. Jinnah, envisaging the ultimate partition of India into the two sovereign States of Pakistan and Hindustan, the former comprising Moslem majority areas of the Punjab, the North-West Frontier, Sind and Baluchistan in the west and of Bengal in the east. Thereafter the achievement of Pakistan became the dominant aim of Mr. Jinnah and the League, and was steadfastly pursued during the discussions with the Cripps Mission in 1942 [on post-war Dominion status], with the British Labour Government after 1945, and in the prolonged inter-party negotiations in India itself.

In January 1946 the long-delayed elections to the Central and Provincial Legislatures were held, at which Mr. Jinnah and the Moslem League made Pakistan an election issue; as a result, the League won all Moslem seats in the Central Legislature and 427 of the 482 Moslem seats in the Provincial Legislatures. In April 1946 began the series of conferences between the British Cabinet Mission, Congress and the Moslem League, and in February 1947 Mr. Clement Attlee, the British Prime Minister, announced the intention of H.M. Government to withdraw every vestige of British authority from India by June 1948. At the same time Lord Mountbatten succeeded Lord Wavell as Viceroy, and on June 3, 1947, announced his plan, discussed with and accepted by the Congress and Moslem League leaders, for the partition of India, subject to the ascertainment of the wishes of the populations in Moslem-majority areas. Resultant plebiscites in those areas showed overwhelming majorities in favour of Pakistan.

THE INDIAN INDEPENDENCE ACT

The Indian Independence Bill, which provided for the establishment of the two independent Dominions of India and Pakistan, had been presented to the British House of Commons on July 4, 1947. Its main provisions were as follows:

(1) The independent Dominions of India and Pakistan would be set up from Aug. 15, 1947.
(2) India would consist of all the territories under the sovereignty of the King which were included in British India, except for those designated as territories of Pakistan.
(3) Pakistan would consist of East Bengal, Western Punjab, Sind and Baluchistan. If the North-West Frontier Province referendum showed a majority for joining the Pakistan Constituent Assembly, that Province too would form part of Pakistan.
(4) There would be a Governor-General appointed by the King for each of the two Dominions, but "unless and until provision is made to the contrary by the Legislature of either of the Dominions, the same person may be Governor-General of both".
(5) From the date of the transfer of power, the British Government would have "no responsibilty for the government of any of the territories now included in British India". The suzerainty of the King over the Indian States would also lapse from the same date.
(6) Temporary provisions were made for the government of the Dominions. The powers of the Legislature of each Dominion, for the purpose of making provisions for its Constitution, would be exercised in the first instance by the Constituent Assembly of that Dominion.
(7) Transitional powers were given to the Viceroy to make such orders as were necessary to bring the Act into force, extending at the latest to March 31, 1948.

The Bill also authorized the establishment of a Pakistan Constituent Assembly under the authority of the Governor-General.

After its second reading in the House of Commons the Bill passed rapidly through the remaining stages in both Houses and received the Royal Assent on July 18, 1947.

AREA AND POPULATION OF PAKISTAN IN 1948

West Pakistan

West Pakistan consisted of the four provinces of West Punjab, North-West Frontier Province, Sind, and Baluchistan. In addition, the principal States to accede to Pakistan were the Rajputana State of Bahawalpur, the Sind State of Khairpur, the Baluch States of Kalat and Las Bela, and Chitral State on the North-West Frontier.

The *West Punjab* was constituted under the Indian Independence Act, 1947, and comprised the western part of the former Punjab province, as defined in Sir Cyril Radcliffe's boundary award [see page 9]. Under that award the districts allotted to Pakistan were (*a*) the Lahore division, with Lahore, Gujranwala, Gurdaspur, Sheikhpura and Sialkot as its main centres; (*b*) the Rawalpindi division, including Rawalpindi, Attock, Jhelum and Shahpur; (*c*) the Multan division, including Multan, Dera Ghazi Khan, Lyallpur, Montgomery and Muzaffargarh. The West Punjab had an area of 62,100 square miles, and 74.7 per cent of its population of 15,800,000 (1941 census) were Moslems.

The *North-West Frontier Province*, incorporated in Pakistan as a result of the referendum in July 1947 [see page 6], consisted of administered and tribal areas, the former with an area of 14,200 square miles and the latter with 24,986 square miles. The province proper had a population in 1941 of 3,038,067, of whom 91 per cent were Moslems, while the tribal areas—which included five States, the most important being Chitral—had an estimated population of 2,500,000.

Sind, which came into existence as a separate entity as a result of the division of Bombay Presidency on April 1, 1936, and became autonomous a year later, had an area (excluding Khairpur State) of

48,136 square miles, and a population (1941 census) of 4,535,000, of whom Moslems numbered 3,208,325.

Baluchistan, which had a total area of 134,002 square miles and a population of 857,835, comprised (*a*) former British Baluchistan proper; (*b*) leased and tribal areas; (*c*) the Baluch States, covering 79,546 square miles, of which Kalat and Las Bela were the most important. The province was predominantly Moslem.

East Pakistan

East Pakistan consisted of East Bengal and the Sylhet district, the following districts of Bengal being awarded to Pakistan under the Indian Independence Act: (*a*) the Chittagong division, with Chittagong, Noakhali and Tippera as the main centres; (*b*) the Dacca division, including Dacca, Faridpur, Bakarganj and Mymensingh; (*c*) the Presidency division, including Jessore and Murshidabad; (*d*) the Rajshahi division, including Rajshahi, Rangpur and Dinajpur. The area of East Bengal was 49,500 square miles, with a total population of 41,910,000.

In an Ordinance issued on March 27, 1955, by the Governor-General, East Bengal was renamed East Pakistan.

Karachi was the capital of Pakistan, and other leading centres were Lahore (West Punjab); Dacca (East Bengal); Rawalpindi (West Punjab); Multan (West Punjab); Sialkot (West Punjab); and Peshawar (North-West Frontier Province). Quetta (Baluchistan) and the port of Chittagong (East Bengal) were also important centres.

ACCESSION OF SEPARATE STATES

Sind

The Sind Legislative Assembly, meeting at Karachi on June 26, 1947, voted by 33 votes to 20 in favour of Sind's union with Pakistan. All Congress party members opposed the motion, which was moved by the Sind Premier. At the same time four members were elected to represent the provinces in the Pakistan Constituent Assembly, three from the Moslem League and one representing Sind minorities.

Baluchistan

A *jirga* (assembly) of all the tribal chiefs of British Baluchistan, meeting on June 29, 1947, also decided by unanimous vote to join Pakistan. Kalat, the largest Indian State in Baluchistan, was not represented at the *jirga*, which in conformity with the Statement of June 3 [see page 7] represented only the British part of the territory; an announcement on April 2, 1948, however, said that Kalat had acceded to Pakistan, which would have control over the State's defence, foreign relations and communications under an instrument of accession signed by the Khan of Kalat. Three of Kalat's feudatory states had earlier acceded to Pakistan, and the accession of Kalat itself came after several weeks' negotiations during which the Khan visited Karachi for conversations with the Governor-General, Mr. Jinnah. Kalat had an area of about 75,000 square miles and a population of over 500,000 (mainly Baluchis, with some Pathans and Sindhis).

In April 1952 the Rulers of the States of Kalat, Las Bela, Makran and Kharan agreed to integrate their territories into a single State Union. The Union was then in June 1954 merged with Baluchistan.

North-West Frontier Province

Polling took place in the North-West Frontier Province on July 6, 1947, on the question of union with Pakistan or India, the final results being overwhelmingly for union with Pakistan, by 289,244 votes to 2,874 (just over half the electorate voting).

Bahawalpur

Bahawalpur State, whose accession to Pakistan was announced on Oct. 7, 1947, was one of the largest Rajputana States. It was adjacent to the Pakistani frontier and had a population—predominantly Moslem—of 1,500,000 and an area of nearly 16,500 square miles.

Frontier States

Since their accession to Pakistan the States of Chitral, Dir and

Swat, which lay on the Afghan border in the extreme north of Pakistan, had been ruled over by their Princes. In July 1969 it was announced that they were to be incorporated in West Pakistan. Two other States, Amb and Hunza, continued to be autonomous.

Assam

The referendum in the Sylhet district of Assam, held on July 6, 1947, resulted in a majority of 55,578 in favour of joining East Bengal, 239,619 votes being cast for union with Pakistan. The Sylhet district covered 5,288 square miles and had a population of about 2,400,000.

Punjab and Bengal

The Punjab Legislative Assembly, meeting on June 23, 1947, decided in favour of the partition of the province. Meeting first in joint session, 91 members (of whom 88 were Moslems) voted in favour of joining a new Constituent Assembly, while 77 (Hindus, Sikhs and Scheduled Caste representatives) voted in favour of entering the existing Constituent Assembly if the Province remained united. The Assembly then split into two sections, the East Punjab section voting by 50 votes to 22 in favour of partition, and although the West Punjab section voted against partition by 69 votes to 27 the former vote ensured the division of the Punjab, since the British plan of June 3, 1947, provided that if a simple majority of either section decided on partition this would take place. This applied also to Bengal. [The plan referred to was that presented to the British House of Commons by the then Prime Minister, Mr. Clement Attlee, and announced the Government's intention to introduce legislation during its current session for the transfer of power, on a Dominion status basis, to one or two successor authorities, leaving it to the Indians themselves to decide whether or not there should be partition.]

The Bengal Legislative Assembly met in two sections on June 20, 1947, to decide on the question of the partition of Bengal. The Hindu-majority section voted in favour by 58 votes to 21, thereby ensuring the division of Bengal under the British plan, while the Moslem-majority section voted against by 106 to 35.

The Governor of Bengal, Sir Frederick Burrows, announced on July 1 that in view of the situation created by the decision to partition Bengal, Ministers would be appointed to the Bengal Government to represent the viewpoint of West Bengal (i.e., the Hindu-majority area, which remained in India). He added that the present Bengal Ministry (i.e., the Moslem League Ministry headed by Mr. Suhrawardy) would be in actual administrative charge of the various portfolios; that the policies it formulated would, however, be implemented only in East Bengal, unless the West Bengal Ministers specifically agreed to their implementation in that part of the province remaining in India; that the new Ministers would be consulted on all questions affecting West Bengal; and that they would have the right to initiate policy in respect of West Bengal, their decisions being implemented by the Government.

Elections took place on July 4-5 in East and West Bengal for nominees to the Constituent Assemblies of India and Pakistan.

In the East Bengal elections to the Pakistan Assembly all 29 Moslem seats were filled by members of the Moslem League, while Congress secured all of the 12 General seats.

Junagadh

The accession to Pakistan on Aug. 18, 1947, of the Kathiawar State of Junagadh, which had been accepted by Pakistan but whose accession was not recognized by India, gave rise to tension between the two Dominions and was strongly opposed in India, and in particular by the other Kathiawar States, on the grounds that Junagadh's adhesion to Pakistan jeopardised the independence and sovereignty of those States.

Junagadh, situated in the south-west of the Kathiawar peninsula, was one of the premier Kathiawar States. It had a population of about 800,000 (of whom over 80 per cent were Hindus and the rest Moslems) and contained enclaves of the territory of other Kathiawar States—e.g. Gondal, Jetpur and Porbandar. Although the population was predominantly Hindu, the Nawab was a Moslem and his *Dewan* and Ministers also Moslems. Junagadh was about 450 miles from Pakistan, having direct access to it by sea but being separated from it geographically by Nawangar and other Kathiawar States (all of which had acceded to India) and by the Rann of Kutch.

Indian troops on Nov. 1, 1947, entered without opposition the small Kathiawar States of Babariawad and Mangrol, both tributaries of Junagadh State. An Indian communiqué stated that the Junagadh authorities were taking "oppressive action" against the people of Babariawad, whose chiefs had announced the accession of that territory to India, and that attempts had been made to force the Babariawad chiefs to denounce the accession to India and substitute for it accession to Pakistan. Following the occupation of Babariawad and Mangrol, Indian troops entered and occupied Junagadh on Nov. 9 in response to a request by the Junagadh Executive Council. The Pakistan Government, which had previously announced its willingness to negotiate on the Junagadh question, sent a protest to India against the "violation of Pakistani territory".

The Indian States Ministry announced on Jan. 15 that the question of the accession of Junagadh, and of Babariawad, Mangrol and other tributary States, would be decided by the "free expression of the wishes of their peoples", a referendum being held for this purpose on Feb. 24, 1948. This resulted in an overwhelming majority in favour of accession to India, 190,779 votes being cast for union with India and only 91 for union with Pakistan. Similar plebiscites in the small tributary States of Junagadh also resulted in large majorities for India.

Boundaries

The award of the Boundary Commissions on the division of Bengal and the Punjab between India and Pakistan was announced on Aug. 17, 1947, by Sir Cyril Radcliffe, chairman of both Commissions. The division was as follows:

In Bengal the new frontier would run approximately north-south from the Himalayan foothills east of Darjeeling to the Ganges delta on the Bay of Bengal, leaving East Bengal in Pakistan and West Bengal in India.

Before partition Bengal had a population of 60,000,000 and an area of 77,000 square miles. Under the award it was estimated that 35.14 per cent of the former Bengali population would be in West Bengal and 64.86 per cent in East Bengal, the proportion of Moslems to the total population in West Bengal being 25 per cent and of non-Moslems in East Bengal 29 per cent.

In the Punjab, a province of 100,000 square miles and 28,000,000 inhabitants, division presented a particularly difficult problem, the final frontier being drawn in an approximately north-east/south-west line across the centre of the province, leaving considerable minorities in both Dominions.

Legislation changing the name of the province of West Punjab to Punjab was passed by the Pakistan Parliament on Jan. 7, 1948. (East Punjab had also been renamed Punjab by the Government of India.)

In Pakistan there were strong criticisms of the award, particularly with regard to the demarcation of the Punjab frontier, Sikh leaders bitterly resenting the fact that a considerable Sikh minority had been left in the Pakistani section.

MASS MOVEMENT OF POPULATION FOLLOWING PARTITION OF THE PUNJAB

During 1946 and 1947, before the partition of India and Pakistan, serious communal disorders accompanied by widespread rioting occurred in a number of provinces, resulting in heavy loss of life. Mahatma Gandhi and Mr. Jinnah issued a joint appeal deploring the use of force and calling on the people to desist from acts of violence, but despite their efforts clashes between Hindus, Sikhs and Moslems during the months from April to July 1947 led to the loss of thousands of lives. In August communal fighting rose to an unprecedented pitch of ferocity, particularly after the Boundary Commission award [see above], and after several weeks of complete lawlessness in which thousands more perished, there ensued a mass migration of populations—of Moslems from East Punjab to Pakistan and of Hindus and Sikhs from West Punjab to India—which constituted one of the biggest population movements in recorded history, involving by the end of 1947 over 8,000,000 people.

By the time of the transfer of power on Aug. 15, a state of virtual civil war prevailed over large parts of the Punjab. Armed gangs carried out murder, looting and arson, all communities suffering heavily. In several villages the Moslem population was reported to have been almost annihilated by Sikh *Jathas* (armed bands). By Aug. 20 a mass movement of the population from the riot-affected areas was in full swing; it was reported from Lahore on that date that, out of 300,000 Hindus and Sikhs formerly resident there, less than 10,000 remained, the rest having fled across the frontier to India. The Indian and British Press estimated that not less than 10,000 people of all communities had been murdered by the end of August, although no reliable figures were available.

The Joint Defence Council for India and Pakistan on Aug. 29 decided to abolish the Punjab Boundary Force (originally set up at the time of partition to maintain law and order in the disputed area) and to replace it by new divisional headquarters, both Indian and Pakistani, which would co-operate closely in providing guards and escorts for refugees and enable both Dominions to assume direct control and responsibility within their respective territories.

On Sept. 3 concerted measures for the restoration of law and order and the protection of refugees both in East and West Punjab were unanimously decided on at a conference in Lahore attended by the Dominion Premiers, Ministers, and high civil and military officials of India and Pakistan and of the East and West Punjab Governments. Both Governments reiterated their determination to restore law and order. The East and West Punjab, it was decided, would assume responsibility for the safety and accommodation of refugees, while evacuations would be organized by the Indian and Pakistani military authorities. Custodians of refugee property would be appointed, evacuees being permitted to take away personal goods and possessions. Immediate measures were taken to implement their decisions.

The great two-way movement of refugees across the Punjab frontier was well under way by the beginning of September 1947. Vast, slow-moving columns—often many miles in length—choked the Punjab roads in both directions, the refugees using every variety of transport, including lorries, carts, bullock-wagons, horse-carriages, and bicycles, laden with all the personal belongings they were able to bring away from their former homes; tens of thousands went on foot, often driving their herds of cattle, sheep and goats before them. Food sent from Delhi was dropped by aircraft at various points of the route, while the Government of India made available several hundred lorries to assist the evacuation. A considerable number of refugees were moved by train.

Before the joint organisation of the exodus by the Indian and Pakistan Governments, the refugee columns were in constant fear of attack by armed marauders, many refugees losing their lives in such attacks along different points of the route, others being robbed, and a number of women and girls being abducted. Consequent on the Indian-Pakistani agreement, however, what was described in Delhi as "one of history's largest mass movements of human beings" started on Sept. 11 when over 400,000 Hindu and Sikh evacuees left their homes in the West Punjab and marched on foot, under Indian and Pakistani military escort and protection, towards the East Punjab. An official Delhi statement of Sept. 16 announced that the MEO (Military Evacuation Organization) had, to that date, moved about 1,000,000 refugees, of whom about 400,000 had moved from the East to the West Punjab and about 600,000 in the reverse direction, and Major-Gen. Chimni, head of the MEO, stated on Oct. 7 that the evacuation was proceeding satisfactorily, with 1,628,000 refugees having already been exchanged between East and West Punjab, 450,000 still on their way, and at least 2,000,000 in the West Punjab awaiting evacuation to India.

The Dominion of India Information Bureau in New Delhi announced on Dec. 20 that, in all, more than 8,500,000 refugees, "the largest migration in history", had crossed the Indian-Pakistani border during the past 4 months, of whom non-Moslems (Hindus and Sikhs) leaving Pakistan accounted for 4,362,000, and Moslems leaving India for about 4,100,000—a movement of over 4,000,000 in each direction. An earlier statement had announced that Hindus and Sikhs were being moved into India *en masse* not only from West Punjab but from other parts of Pakistan such as Sind, Baluchistan and the Frontier Province, and that on an average more than 60,000 non-Moslems had been brought across the frontier in safety every day by using all available means of transport.

Although the road columns of refugees suffered, apart from a few isolated instances, little or no molestation from armed bands after the organisation of the exodus by the Indian and Pakistan Governments, several attacks were made on the "refugee specials" carrying large numbers of evacuees by rail, involving heavy loss of life among refugee passengers.

One feature of the mass migration was the transfer by the British Overseas Airways Corporation of 35,000 people from Pakistan to India between Oct. 20 and Nov. 30, and the moving during August of 7,000 Moslem Government officials and their families from Delhi to Pakistan.

By the first week of September some 200,000 non-Moslem refugees had arrived in Delhi, where they subsequently took frequent retaliatory action against Moslems for the seizure of their own property in the West Punjab. On Sept. 8 Delhi was proclaimed a "dangerous area". Energetic action to restore order, and the arrival of troop reinforcements in the city, finally led to an easing of the tension. The numbers killed in the disturbances were estimated at over 1,000.

The mass movement of over 8,000,000 refugees created resettlement and rehabilitation problems of the greatest magnitude both in India and Pakistan. On both sides of the Punjab frontier entire villages and large areas of productive land had been left abandoned by their former occupiers, while in the towns and cities—e.g., Lahore and Multan—many shops and businesses were left tenantless through the removal of their owners to the other Dominion. Both the East and West Punjab Provincial Governments made intensive efforts to resettle the new immigrant population on land vacated by the emigrants.

THE "PATHANISTAN" ISSUE

In the North-West Frontier Province the Government was faced with a movement demanding the secession of the Pathan areas from the province. This movement, the "Redshirt" organization founded by Khan Abdul Ghaffar Khan, boycotted the referendum of July 6, 1947 (resulting in an overwhelming majority for the province's union with Pakistan—see page 6). On Sept. 16, 1947, the "Redshirt" organization was declared illegal by the Provincial Government.

Khan Abdul Ghaffar Khan, however, declared in the Constituent Assembly, of which he was a member, on March 5, 1948, that, though he had opposed partition, he and his followers were loyal to Pakistan but still aspired to an autonomous "Pathanistan" within the Dominion.

On March 8, 1948, he issued an manifesto announcing the formation of a Pakistan People's Party which had as its objective the establishment of a "union of free socialist republics" in Pakistan.

On June 15, 1948, he was arrested for having, with agents of the Fakir of Ipi (a Waziristan tribal leader who had been involved in local risings), tried "to create disturbances to synchronize with the expected advance of the Indian Army" towards Pakistan's frontier, and for having "invited people to rise against the lawfully established Government of the country". On June 16 Khan Abdul Ghaffar Khan was sentenced to three years' imprisonment.

After further arrests of followers of his party and of the Fakir of Ipi, the Provincial Government on July 8, 1948, assumed extraordinary powers by ordinance to deal with persons and organizations suspected of subversive activities.

INAUGURAL MEETING OF THE CONSTITUENT ASSEMBLY—KARACHI PROCLAIMED CAPITAL

The setting up of a Constituent Assembly for Pakistan had been announced from New Delhi on July 26, 1947, prior to the transfer of power, in a statement from the office of the Governor-General. It was provided that the Pakistan Constituent Assembly should consist of 69 members as follows: 41 from East Bengal (29 Moslems and 12 general), 17 from West Punjab (12 Moslems, 3 Hindus, 2 Sikhs), 4 from Sind (3 Moslems, 1 general), 3 from the N.W. Frontier Province (Moslems), 3 from the Sylhet district of Assam (Moslems), and 1 from Baluchistan (Moslem), the members from Sind, the Frontier Province and Baluchistan being those elected to the Indian Constituent Assembly before partition.

The Constituent Assembly met for the first time on Aug. 10 in Karachi, Mr. Jinnah being unanimously elected President of the Assembly (combining that function with the Governor-Generalship) on Aug. 11.

The Assembly on May 23, 1948, adopted a resolution presented by the Government formally proclaiming Karachi, the capital of Sind, as capital of the Dominion of Pakistan. (Karachi had been the provisional capital of the Dominion since the latter came into existence.) This met with strong dissatisfaction on the part of the Sind Moslem League Council, which, on June 11, instructed the Sind Government not to surrender to the Central Government any of its powers in respect of Karachi and to convene a special session of the Sind Legislative Assembly to record a formal denunciation of the Constituent Assembly's resolution, which it was said had "flouted the will of the Sind people". It was not until July 6 that, after having put their views directly before Governor-General Jinnah, the Sind Moslem League Assembly Party decided to acquiesce in the Constituent Assembly's decision. The administration of Karachi, including the air and sea ports, the railway headquarters, and islands off the coast, was formally transferred from the Government of Sind to the Government of Pakistan on July 23.

[In August 1960 Rawalpindi replaced Karachi as the capital of Pakistan, Karachi from then on being known as the Federal Territory of Karachi.]

DEATH OF MR. JINNAH

Mr. Mohammed Ali Jinnah, Govenor-General and creator of Pakistan, died in Karachi from heart failure on Sept. 11, 1948, aged 71.

Mohammed Ali Jinnah was born in Karachi on Dec. 25, 1876. He matriculated at Bombay University, came to London to study law and in 1896 qualified for the Bar. Returning to India, he went into practice in Bombay and entered politics, becoming a member of the Indian National Congress, at that time the only all-India political organization which stood for the attainment of self-government by constitutional means. In 1909 he was elected by the Bombay Presidency Moslem constituency to the newly-constituted Supreme Legislative Council, and in 1913 was returned to the Central Legislature, where he continued to sit until 1945.

Mr. Jinnah, while remaining a member of Congress, joined in 1913 the All-India Moslem League, which had been founded in 1906 for the advancement and protection of Moslem interests and for the promotion of communal harmony. As President of the Moslem League session held in Lucknow in 1916, he played a prominent part in drawing up the "Lucknow Pact" under which Congress and the League reached, for the time being, a settlement of outstanding controversies. In 1920, however, the Congress party adopted Mr. Gandhi's programme of non-violent non-co-operation, and Mr. Jinnah, an opponent of Gandhi's religio-political tactics, resigned from Congress. Nevertheless, as an influential member of the Moslem League, he continued his efforts for Congress-Moslem understanding on outstanding questions, and in 1928 associated himself with the All-Parties Conference held in Bombay. A committee of this conference adopted the "Nehru report" which outlined a plan for Dominion status, and rejected the "14 points" put forward by Mr. Jinnah embodying demands for constitutional safeguards for the Moslem community. On Jan. 1, 1929, however, the "14 points"—including *inter alia* a Federal constitution with residuary powers for the Provinces, the creation of the new Provinces of Sind and Baluchistan, provincial autonomy, and separate electorates—were adopted by the largest representative gathering of Indian Moslems yet held, meeting in New Delhi under the chairmanship of the Aga Khan.

Mr. Jinnah was a delegate to the London Round-Table Conferences of 1930–1931, in which he stood firmly by his 14-point programme, and from 1930 to 1934 was resident in England, practising at the Privy Council Bar. On his return to India in 1934, convinced that the ultimate aim of the Congress party was Hindu domination over the whole of India, he reunited the dissident groups in the Moslem League into an active and united organization, of which he became permanent President, representative of the Moslems of India as a whole. Thereafter the League rapidly advanced in influence and membership, particularly in the Moslem-majority provinces.

Mr. Jinnah's successor as Governor-General of Pakistan was Khwaja Nazimuddin, the Premier of East Bengal, who took the oath on Sept. 14, 1948.

II. EFFORTS AT FORMULATION OF A CONSTITUTION, 1949-1954

The Pakistan Constituent Assembly began preparatory work in 1949 on the formulation of a Constitution, on which the new State of Pakistan would be based. Due, however, to internal developments, culminating in 1954 in the dissolution of the Constituent Assembly and the imposition of a state of emergency, work on the Constitution was resumed only in the first half of 1955 with the election of a new Assembly.

By the time the Constituent Assembly was dissolved in 1954, a draft Constitution had been completed.

PREPARATORY WORK ON THE CONSTITUTION

The Pakistan Constituent Assembly on Oct. 7, 1953, opened a general debate on the report of the Basic Principles Committee which had been appointed in 1949 to prepare a draft Constitution [see below]. After a prolonged and detailed discussion of the report, it was subsequently decided on Nov. 2 that Pakistan should become an Islamic Republic within the British Commonwealth. The Committee's report (the third which it had issued) and the debates in the Assembly marked an important stage in the development of Pakistan's future Constitution, which had been the subject of controversy for over four years, the main questions at issue being (*a*) the basis of representation of East and West Pakistan in the Federal Legislature, and (b) the "Islamic" nature of the State. The principal stages in the working out of the Constitution are dealt with below.

THE OBJECTIVES RESOLUTION

The Basic Principles Committee was appointed on March 12, 1949, by the Assembly, which adopted at the same time a resolution defining the objectives of the Constitution moved by Mr. Liaquat Ali Khan, the Prime Minister. The resolution provided *inter alia*:

(1) That the principles of democracy, freedom, equality, tolerance and social justice, as enunciated by Islam, should be fully observed.

(2) That Moslems should be enabled to order their lives in accordance with the teachings and requirements of Islam.

(3) That adequate provision should be made for minorities to profess and practise their religions freely and to develop their cultures.

(4) That adequate provision should be made to safeguard the legitimate interests of minorities and of backward and depressed classes.

(5) That fundamental rights, including equality of status and of opportunity, social, economic, and political justice, and freedom of thought, expression, belief, faith, worship, and association, subject to law and public morality, should be guaranteed.

(6) That the independence of the Judiciary should be fully secured.

FIRST AND SECOND REPORTS OF BASIC PRINCIPLES COMMITTEE

The main recommendations of the first interim report of the Committee, presented to the Assembly on Sept. 28, 1950, were as follows:

(1) The executive power would be vested in the Head of State, acting on the advice of the Ministry.

(2) The Head of State would appoint a Prime Minister, the other Ministers being then appointed on the Prime Minister's advice.

(3) The Federal Legislature would consist of the House of Units (elected by the Provincial Legislature) and the House of the People (directly elected). The two Houses would have equal powers, but would under certain circumstances meet in joint session.

(4) Bills passed by the Legislature would be presented to the Head of State, who would either declare his assent or return the Bill.

(5) Each province would have a unicameral Legislature elected

for five years. Executive power would be exercised by the Head of the province.

(6) Subjects for legislation would be divided into those reserved for the Federal Legislature, those reserved for the Provincial Legislature, and a concurrent list of subjects which might be dealt with by either. In the case of conflict between Federal and Provincial laws the former would prevail.

(7) The Head of the State might proclaim an emergency and suspend the Constitution in whole or in part.

(8) The official language of the State would be Urdu.

The interim report aroused strong opposition from many sections of public opinion. In East Pakistan, which contained over half the population of the country, the proposal to grant the House of Units (in which all the provinces would have equal representation) equal powers with the House of the People, which would be elected on a population basis, was attacked as "designedly framed to cripple East Pakistan", and led to widespread protest meetings and demonstrations in which officials of the Moslem League (the Government party) took a prominent part. Objection was also taken in East Pakistan to the choice of Urdu as the official language, to the exclusion of Bengali. Both in East Pakistan and the Punjab, the second largest province, the Constitution was criticized as giving the Federal Government too much power at the expense of the provinces, as granting the Head of the State excessive emergency powers, and as failing to provide adequate safeguards against their abuse. Finally, the Mullahs (Moslem religious teachers) denounced the proposed Constitution as insufficiently Islamic. In view of the opposition aroused, the Government subsequently withdrew the report for further consideration.

A revised report was presented to the Constituent Assembly on Dec. 22, 1952, by Khwaja Nazimuddin (who had succeeded Mr. Liaquat Ali Khan after the latter's assassination on Oct. 16, 1951), proposing a number of major changes intended both to give the draft Constitution a more Islamic character and to meet the objections raised in East Pakistan. The main proposals of this report were:

(1) The Head of the State must be a Moslem.
(2) There would be parity of representation between East and West Pakistan in both the House of Units (120 members) and the

House of the People (400 members). The units composing West Pakistan would be represented in each House in proportion to their population.

(3) Religious minorities would have separate representation in the Federal and Provincial Legislatures. In the House of the People there would be 21 caste Hindus (20 from East Pakistan and one from Sind), 26 Scheduled Caste representatives (24 from East Pakistan and two from Sind), three Christians (one from East Pakistan and two from the Punjab), two Buddhists from East Pakistan, and one Parsee from Karachi.

(4) The House of the People and the Provincial Legislatures would be elected by secret ballot by all citizens over 21.

(5) The representation of Kashmir and Junagadh in the House of Units and House of the People would be determined by the Federal Legislature, but would not affect the parity between East and West Pakistan.

(6) The Cabinet would be responsible only to the House of the People.

(7) The Head of the State would appoint a board of five persons versed in Islamic law to advise on legislation, similar boards being set up in each province. If at any stage during the passage of a Bill a member of Parliament objected that it violated the tenets of the Koran and the Sunna, the Bill would be referred to the board; if the board reached a unanimous decision the Bill would be referred back to Parliament for reconsideration in the light of their report. Parliament's final decision would require a majority both of the members of Parliament and of the Moslem members.

(8) The existing Federal Court would be replaced by a Supreme Court consisting of seven judges appointed by the Head of the State, which would hear all appeals, including those hitherto remitted to the Privy Council.

(9) The decision on the official language of the State would be referred to the Constituent Assembly.

This report also met with strong opposition. In West Pakistan, and especially in the Punjab, the suggested parity between East and West Pakistan was criticized because, it was argued, it would enable the former to dominate the Legislature. Strong objections were also raised to the proposed religious advisory board, it being pointed out that the board would virtually have power to veto any legislation. Moreover, the minorities considered the stipulation that the Head of the State must be a Moslem as unnecessary and offensive.

When the Assembly met to consider the report on Jan. 21, 1953,

Mr. Nazimuddin announced that he did not propose to move the legislation but intended first to consult leaders of public opinion on points of disagreement.

DIRECTIVE PRINCIPLES OF STATE POLICY

The Basic Principles Committee accompanied its report with the following list of recommendations for Directive Principles of State Policy.

(1) The State should be guided by the principles of the Objectives Resolution of March 12, 1949 [see page 18].

(2) Steps should be taken to enable Moslems to order their lives in accordance with the Koran and the Sunna [*inter alia* the compulsory teaching of the Koran, prohibition of drinking, gambling and prostitution, and proper organization of mosques].

(3) An organization should be set up for making the teaching of Islam known to the people.

(4) Existing laws should be brought into conformity with Islamic principles, and such injunctions of the Koran and the Sunna as could be given legislative effect should be codified.

(5) Activities subversive of the principles of the Objectives Resolution should be forbidden.

(6) The provision of food, clothing, housing, education and medical relief for citizens incapable of earning their livelihood owing to unemployment, sickness, or similar reasons.

(7) The improvement of living standards, the prevention of the concentration of wealth and means of production in the hands of a few, and the prevention of the exploitation of the workers and peasants.

(8) Abolition of illiteracy as rapidly as possible.

(9) Training and education for the population of different areas, to enable them to participate fully in all forms of national activity and service.

(10) Discouragement of parochial, tribal and racial feelings among Moslems.

(11) Strengthening of the bonds of unity between Moslem countries.

(12) Promotion of peace and goodwill among the peoples of the world.

(13) Only a person possessing ability, character and piety, and fit to conduct the affairs of the State in accordance with the Objectives Resolution, should be elected as Head of the State.

(14) Separation of the Judiciary from the Executive within three years.

(15) Protection for all legitimate rights and interests of the non-Moslem communities.

(16) Protection of children, young people and women against exploitation and employment in unsuitable occupations.

FUNDAMENTAL RIGHTS COMMITTEE

The Constituent Assembly adopted on Oct. 6, 1950, the report of a committee appointed to draw up a definition of fundamental rights. The provisions of this report, which was intended as a preamble to the Constitution, were as follows:

(1) All citizens were equal before the law and entitled to the equal protection of the law.

(2) No person should be deprived of life or liberty save in accordance with the law.

(3) No person should be punished for an act which was not punishable when it was committed.

(4) The right to apply for a writ of *habeas corpus* should not be suspended, except in the case of an external or internal threat to the security of the State or other grave emergency.

(5) There should be no discrimination on grounds of religion, race, caste, sex or place of birth with regard to access to places of public entertainment, recreation, welfare or utility.

(6) All forms of slavery, servitude, forced labour, torture, or cruel or inhuman treatment or punishment were declared illegal.

(7) The employment of children under 14 in factories or mines, or in occupations involving danger to life or injury to health, was prohibited.

(8) All duly qualified citizens were made eligible for appointment in the service of the State, irrespective of religion, race, caste, sex, descent or place of birth, provided that it should not be unlawful for the State to reserve posts in favour of any minority or backward section.

(9) No person should be deprived of his property without adequate compensation.

(10) All citizens were guaranteed: (*a*) freedom of speech, expression, association, occupation, acquisition and disposal of property, and peaceful assembly; (*b*) the right to move freely throughout Pakistan and to reside in any part of the country; (*c*) the right to equal pay for equal work.

(11) Freedom of conscience and the right to profess, practise and

propagate any religion, subject to public order and morality, were guaranteed.

(12) No person attending any educational institution should be required to receive religious instruction or to attend religious worship other than that of his own community or denomination. No religious community should be prevented from providing religious instruction for pupils of that community in any educational institution which it maintained. No person should be compelled to pay any special taxes the proceeds of which were specifically appropriated for the propagation or maintenance of any religion other than his own.

(13) "The notion of untouchability being inconsistent with human dignity, its practice is declared unlawful."

Another report, presented on Dec. 22, 1952, by the Fundamental Rights Committee, supported the Basic Principles Committee's proposal for separate electorates and also proposed that both the Federal Government and each Provincial Government should include a Minister for Minority Affairs.

REPRESENTATION IN FEDERAL LEGISLATURE

It was announced on Oct. 3, 1953, that agreement had finally been reached on a basis of representation in the Federal Legislature, as follows:

(*a*) As regards the composition of the Upper House, Pakistan would be divided into five units (of which East Pakistan would be one), each with 10 members. (*b*) The Lower House of 300 members would be elected on a population basis, the members from East Pakistan thereby being in a majority. (*c*) In the Federal Legislature as a whole, the total number of members from East and West Pakistan would be equal, East Pakistan having 10 members in the Upper House and 165 in the Lower, and West Pakistan 40 in the Upper House and 135 in the Lower House. The allotment of seats in the two Houses is shown in the table.

	Lower House	Upper House
East Pakistan	165	10
The Punjab	75	10
N.W. Frontier Province, Frontier States, and Tribal Areas	24	10
Sind and Khairpur	19	10
Baluchistan, Baluchistan States Union, Bahawalpur, and Karachi	17	10

The Head of State and the Prime Minister would be from different zones, i.e. one from West Pakistan and the other from East Pakistan.

On Oct. 27, 1953, the Constituent Assembly adopted the preamble to the Basic Principles Committee's report, embodying the Objectives Resolution of 1949 [see page 18], and on Oct. 30 approved a provision that no future Legislature should enact any law repugnant to the Koran and the Sunna.

An amendment to the Basic Principles Committee's report, changing the official name of the State from Pakistan to "the Islamic Republic of Pakistan", and providing that the Head of State should bear the title of President, was adopted on Nov. 2, after the 12 Congress members and two Scheduled Caste representatives had withdrawn from the Assembly.

AMENDMENTS TO THE CONSTITUTION

A Bill amending the Constitution was published by the Pakistan Government on July 29, 1954, its provisions being as follows:

(1) The Constituent Assembly was empowered to amend the Indian Independence Act, 1947 [see page 3], and to assume powers to assert its sovereign character, including the power to make a Constitution for Pakistan not merely as a Dominion but as an independent Republic.

(2) The Constituent Assembly's competence to make provision for the Constitution of the Dominion of Pakistan would include power to make constitutional provisions for the entire territory of Pakistan—i.e., including those States which had acceded to Pakistan in accordance with the Government of India Act, 1935.

(3) The Constituent Assembly's competence to make constitutional provisions applicable to the entire territory of Pakistan could not be called in question in any court. This provision amended the Government of India Act, 1935, under which the Pakistan Federal Court had been empowered to interpret the Instrument of Accession in relation to any State which had acceded to Pakistan, and to give a declaratory judgment on any questions arising out of such an interpretation.

[Under the terms of the Instruments of Accession signed by the Rulers of those States which acceded to Pakistan after the achievement of independence, the changes made by the new Bill became binding upon the Rulers of those States—i.e., no court of law could in future question the powers exercised by the Constituent Assembly in relation to those States.]

The Bill was passed on Aug. 2 and enacted under the name of the Constitution (Amendment) Act, 1954.

POLITICAL DEVELOPMENTS DURING 1953

In 1953 Pakistan suffered a grave food shortage and economic upheaval, culminating in widespread unrest and riots in February and March which led to a political crisis.

The Food Crisis. Khwaja Nazimuddin, the Prime Minister, gave details of the food situation at a press conference on April 9, 1953, and announced that the Government had approached the United States for assistance in the form of 1,000,000 tons of wheat, to avoid a worsening of the situation, especially in parts of the Punjab where food shortages were particularly serious. In addition to the inadequacy or failure of rainfall, Mr. Nazimuddin attributed the food shortage partly to the fact that supplies of water in Indian-controlled canals [see pages 52–58] had been considerably lower than even the water shortage resulting from natural causes would have justified; other contributory causes included the diversion of cash crops of some areas previously under wheat; hoarding; and damage to crops by locusts.

The Economy. The serious deterioration in the country's economic situation developed partly because of a severe shrinkage in the world demand for jute and cotton (Pakistan's principal exports) and partly because of two years of virtual drought, aggravated by swarms of locusts in the Punjab, which had precipitated the food shortage. Pakistan's foreign exchange reserves had fallen to a dangerously low level during 1952, and in February 1953 imports were drastically cut, with the result that prices rose sharply. In order to meet this situation, the Legislative Assembly granted the Government on March 26 extraordinary powers, for a period of two years, to control the price, production and distribution of any commodity which was declared by the Government to be "essential". The food shortage and rising prices led to widespread unrest, which was exploited by religious extremists to foment the riots of February and March.

The Communal Riots. Serious rioting occurred in Karachi, Lahore,

Rawalpindi and other Pakistani towns in February and March 1953 after Moslem demands that the unorthodox Ahmadiya sect (which tended to interpret Islam in rational terms calculated to appeal to the modern world, and was therefore regarded as heretical by conservative Moslems) should be declared a non-Moslem minority and that its members, including the Foreign Minister (Sir Muhammad Zafrulla Khan), should be dismissed from government posts. The Government arrested 11 leaders of the All-Moslem Parties' Convention early on Feb. 27, following the Convention's decision to launch "direct action", and issued a statement attributing the agitation to the Ahrars, a religious political movement. Anti-Ahmadiya demonstrations took place in Karachi on Feb. 27–28 and on March 7, and violent rioting broke out at Lahore on March 4–5, spreading to Rawalpindi where a general strike took place. Disturbances also occurred in the Punjab, but by March 11 the situation generally had returned to normal.

Mr. Nazimuddin's Government was widely accused of indecision and of failure to take the firm action necessary to cope with the economic situation and to maintain public order. Moreover, allegations had also been made that the efficiency of the administration was being undermined by nepotism and by provincial jealousies. The Governor-General therefore called on Mr. Mohammed Ali (then Pakistan Ambassador to the United States) to form a new Government, and on April 17, 1953, a new Cabinet was announced which included six of the 11 members of the outgoing Government. Mr. Mohammed Ali himself became Prime Minister.

Mr. Nazimuddin, in a statement issued on April 18, described the Governor-General's dismissal of the Cabinet as "illegal and unconstitutional", on the ground that all the provisions of the Government of India Act giving the Governor-General discretionary powers had ceased to have effect with the enforcement of the Indian Independence Act of 1947 [see page 3], by which the Dominion of Pakistan was constituted. He nevertheless declared: "The serious situation through which Pakistan is passing demands that I should not do anything which will in the least weaken the position within the country or in the world."

The Chief Minister of the Punjab, Mr. Daultana, tendered his resignation and that of his Cabinet on March 24 at the request of

Mr. Nazimuddin, acting in his capacity as President of the Moslem League (from which he later resigned, being succeeded by Mr. Mohammed Ali). During the recent religious disturbances in the Punjab, Mr. Daultana had announced the Provincial Government's support for the rioters' demands; although he had subsequently retracted this support he had been widely accused of having instigated the riots for political reasons, and on April 10 he resigned from the presidency of the Punjab Moslem League.

A new Punjab Cabinet was formed on April 3 by Mr. Firoz Khan Noon (Governor of East Bengal), who took the post of Chief Minister.

DISSOLUTION OF CONSTITUENT ASSEMBLY

A further political crisis, culminating in the dissolution of the Constituent Assembly by the Governor-General, Mr. Ghulam Mohammed, and the proclamation of a state of emergency, was precipitated in September–October 1954 on the one hand by differences inside the Moslem League and the Constituent Assembly over the provisions of the draft Constitution, and on the other by disagreements between the Governor-General and the dominant section of the Assembly.

The main constitutional problems at issue were those of the relationship between the Central Government and the provinces, and of the representation of the provinces in the Central Legislature, on which the following four main views were put forward:

(1) The "East Bengal group", which commanded a majority inside the Moslem League Assembly Party, supported the compromise proposals on representation in the Federal Legislature which had been put forward in 1953 [see page 23] and which were to have been incorporated in the draft Constitution.

(2) The "Punjab group" feared that these proposals would give East Bengal a dominant position, and therefore advocated that the Federal Government's powers should be limited to the fields of defence, foreign affairs, currency and exchange, foreign trade, and interzonal communications. In order to strengthen West Pakistan's position, they favoured the amalgamation of the Western provinces into either a "zonal subfederation" (the policy supported by the Chief Minister of the Punjab, Mr. Firoz Khan Noon) or a single unit (as proposed by Mr. Mian Mumtaz Daultana, his predecessor). The Governor-General was believed to be sympathetic to the group's aims.

(3) A majority of members of the Sind Assembly, led by the

Chief Minister (Pirzada Abdus Sattar, a strong supporter of Mr. Mohammed Ali), favoured a unicameral Federal Legislature in which all the provinces would have equal representation.

(4) Dr. Khan Sahib (the Minister of Communications) had advocated a unitary form of government, with a single legislature elected on a population basis, but had favoured the unification of West Pakistan as an intermediate stage if necessary.

A draft resolution passed by the Assembly on Sept. 16 gave the Federation sole powers to deal with a large number of subjects, including defence, foreign affairs, foreign trade, currency and exchange, communications (except inland navigation, broadcasting and television), industrial development, and exploitation of mineral resources. The subjects reserved for the provinces (the "provincial list") included, *inter alia,* inland navigation, flood control, irrigation, and electric power. Among subjects on the "concurrent list" (on which both the Federation and the provinces might legislate) were broadcasting, refugee rehabilitation, labour, welfare, unemployment and social insurance. It was stipulated (*a*) that Federal laws should prevail over provincial legislation in case of conflict; and (*b*) that all disputes between the Federation and the provinces, or between the provinces themselves, for which the Supreme Court had not been given original jurisdiction, should be brought before a tribunal to be set up by the Chief Justice at the request of any of the parties concerned. In such disputes the tribunal's report would be sent to the President for a final decision.

On Sept. 21 the Assembly adopted without opposition an amendment to the Government of India Act (1935) sponsored by the Government and supported by the "East Bengal group", which provided (1) that the Governor-General should appoint as Prime Minister "the member of the Federal Legislature who commands the confidence of the majority of the members of the Federal Legislature"; (2) that Ministers, Ministers of State and Deputy Ministers should be appointed from among the members of the Federal Legislature; (3) that "the Council of Ministers shall be collectively responsible to the Federal Legislature, and Ministers, including the Prime Minister, shall cease to hold office on the expression of want of confidence by the Federal Legislature"; (4) that "the Governor-General shall be bound by the advice of the Ministers".

The Bill (which passed through the Assembly in 15 minutes during Mr. Ghulam Mohammed's absence) terminated the position whereby Ministers had held office "during the pleasure" of the Governor-General. It thus made impossible a repetition of the events in 1953, when Mr. Ghulam Mohammed dismissed Mr. Nazimuddin's Cabinet despite the fact that it had received a vote of confidence in the Assembly shortly beforehand, and appointed Mr. Mohammed Ali as Prime Minister although the latter was not at the time a member of the Assembly [see page 26].

Another controversial measure adopted by the Assembly on Sept. 21 was the repeal of the Public and Representative Offices (Disqualification) Act of 1949—generally referred to as PRODA. The Bill permitted the Governor-General to debar from public life, for a maximum period of 10 years, Ministers, members of the Central and Provincial Legislatures, and Parliamentary Secretaries found guilty of corruption, maladministration or any abuse of official position. The Bill repealing the Act laid down, however, that it would not affect penalties already imposed, or any cases pending before the courts.

Finally, the Assembly approved on the same day the report of the Basic Principles Committee with only minor amendments, despite strong protests from Congress party members who contended that the report involved discrimination against the minorities. The Assembly then adjourned until Oct. 27 to enable the Bill embodying the new Constitution, on the basis of the decisions previously taken, to be drawn up for final consideration.

DECLARATION OF STATE OF EMERGENCY

During the following weeks, however, while Mr. Mohammed Ali was absent in the United States, a crisis developed as a result of the differences between the "Punjab group" and the "East Bengal group". The Working Committee of the Moslem League, meeting on Oct. 22, 1954, decided to postpone the party convention—which had been fixed for Oct. 31—"in view of the strained political atmosphere in the country". On Oct. 23, after discussions between leading politicians belonging to the "Punjab group", the Punjab Moslem League Assembly Party unanimously adopted a resolution demanding (*a*) the restriction of the Federal Government's powers to the five subjects of defence, foreign affairs, currency and exchange, foreign trade and interzonal communications; (*b*) the formation of a committee representing the units of West Pakistan to decide upon the subjects "of common interest to the Western units" and the administrative and legislative machinery to deal with them; and (*c*) the incorporation in the Constitution of machinery for its amendment within five years. A majority of the Sind Moslem League Assembly Party, however, issued a statement on the same day strongly opposing the proposed zonal subfederation, and demanding the adoption of the Constitution as drafted by Dec. 25.

In view of these developments, Mr. Mohammed Ali returned to Karachi, and on Oct. 24 the Governor-General of Pakistan issued a declaration proclaiming a state of emergency and declaring that the Constituent Assembly could "no longer function" (a phrase variously interpreted as meaning either prorogation *sine die* or immediate dissolution). At the same time Mr. Mohammed Ali was asked to reconstitute his Government and the Cabinet was reduced from 11 to 10 members, all the Ministers belonging to the Moslem League with the exception of Major-General Iskander Mirza, General Ayub Khan and Dr. Khan Sahib.

PROVINCIAL DEVELOPMENTS 1951–1954

Moslem League Gains in Punjab and North-West Frontier Province

Elections to the Punjab Legislative Assembly, the first elections held in Pakistan since the foundation of the State, took place between March 10 and 20, 1951, and resulted in a victory for the Moslem League. 30 per cent of the electorate voted, and the results were as follows: Moslem League, 143 seats; Jinnah-Awami League, 31 seats; Independents, 16 seats; *Azad* Pakistan Party and *Jamaat-i-Islami,* one seat each; and minorities, 5 seats. The Moslem League represented 47 per cent of the votes cast, or 14 per cent of the electorate.

Following the elections, Mr. Daultana, leader of the Moslem League group in the Assembly, formed a new Cabinet, this being the first formed in the Punjab since January 1949 when the province was brought under Governor's rule.

Elections to the North-West Frontier Province Legislative Assembly were held between Nov. 26 and Dec. 12, 1951, and also resulted in a Moslem League victory. The two chief Opposition parties, the Jinnah-Awami League and the "Redshirts" [see page 13], reached an agreement not to put up candidates against each other; the "Redshirts", who were banned in the province, did not, however, contest the elections as an organization, but put forward a number of candidates standing as Independents. The results were as follows: Moslem League, 67; Independent Moslems, 13; Jinnah-Awami League, four; non-Moslem, one. The Independent deputies and the non-Moslems all applied for Moslem League membership after the elections, leaving the four Jinnah-Awami League members as the only Opposition.

Moslem League Losses in East Bengal

Provincial elections held in East Bengal (East Pakistan) from March 8–11, 1954, resulted in an overwhelming victory for the United Front (*Juqta*), an alliance of parties opposed to the ruling Moslem League. Out of 309 seats, the United Front (consisting of three Moslem parties—the Awami Moslem League, the *Krishak Sramik* Party and the *Nizam-i-Islam*) gained 237 seats; the Moslem League, 10; Independents, 3; *Khilafat-e-Rabani,* 1; and minorities, 72.

The main items in the United Front's programme were as follows: (1) Recognition of Bengali as an official language on a par with Urdu. (2) Rejection of the draft Constitution, the dissolution of the Constituent Assembly, and its replacement by a directly elected body. (3) Complete autonomy for East Pakistan in all matters except defence, foreign policy and currency, which would be reserved to the Central Legislature. (4) Complete freedom from the Centre with regard to export of jute. (5) Consultation between the Centre and East Pakistan on the allocation of foreign exchange for imports. (6) Abolition of the Indo-Pakistani passport and visa system and of existing restrictions on trade between East and West Bengal. (7) Devaluation of the Pakistani rupee.

About 65 per cent of the electorate went to the polls, in which all five members of the outgoing Moslem League lost their seats.

The defeat of the Moslem League in East Bengal, which contained 56 per cent of the total population of Pakistan, led to demands for the resignation of the Central Government and the dissolution of the Constituent Assembly as unrepresentative. These demands, however, were rejected by Mr. Mohammed Ali, who stated: "The task of framing the Constitution was not entrusted to the Moslem League as such, but to all members, Moslem or non-Moslem, specifically chosen for this purpose. There is no Government party and no Opposition in the Constituent Assembly." For members from a particular province to resign merely because their party had gone out of office in that province would, he argued, create an unworkable precedent. Elections to one or other of the Provincial Legislatures would be held practically every year, and if the character of the Central Government changed whenever a new party came to power in one of the provinces, there would be no stability or continuity.

Following the Prime Minister's statement, the Working Committee of the Moslem League accordingly ordered its members from East Bengal in the Constituent Assembly not to resign their seats.

On March 25, 1954, Mr. Fazlul Huq (the leader of the *Krishak Sramik* Party), who had previously stated that he would make a point of preserving the best possible relations with Karachi provided that satisfaction was given on the issues of language [see below], the Constitution and provincial autonomy, was called upon to form a new Government in East Bengal.

The Language Controversy

The question of the official language or languages of Pakistan had given rise to vigorous controversy in different parts of the country. Although Mr. Jinnah and Mr. Liaquat Ali Khan had advocated that Urdu should be the official language, more than half of Pakistan's population of 75,000,000 was concentrated in East Bengal, where Bengali was the predominant language (other widely spoken languages in Pakistan being Pushtu, particularly in the North-West Frontier Province, and Sindhi). Whereas it was widely felt in West Pakistan that Urdu should be the only official language, public opinion in East Pakistan was equally insistent that Bengali should be recognized as an official language on the same footing as Urdu.

A decision that Urdu and Bengali should be the official languages of Pakistan had been taken by the Moslem League Parliamentary Party on April 20, 1954, and had led to widespread anti-Bengali demonstrations in Karachi on April 22–23. While many shopkeepers declared a *hartal* in protest against the official recognition of Bengali, some 5,000 demonstrators marched on the Parliament building and demonstrated in favour of their demand that Urdu should be the only recognized language.

The Pakistan Constituent Assembly, meeting on May 7, 1954, approved a "language formula" embodying the following eight resolutions:

(1) The official languages of the Islamic Republic of Pakistan would be Urdu and Bengali, together with "such other provincial languages as may be declared to be such by the Head of State on the recommendation of the Provincial Legislatures concerned".
(2) Members of Parliament would have the right to speak in Urdu and Bengali as well as in English.
(3) For a period of 20 years from the coming into force of Pakistan's Constitution, the English language would continue to be used "for all official purposes of the Republic for which it was being used immediately before such coming into force", notwithstanding resolutions (1) and (2) above.
(4) All provincial languages would be placed on an equal footing as regards examinations for the Central services.
(5) Provision would be made for the teaching of Arabic, Urdu, and Bengali in secondary schools to enable students to take one or two of them, in addition to the language used as the medium of instruction.
(6) The State would take "all measures for the development and growth of a common national language".
(7) A Commission would be appointed ten years after the coming into force of the Constitution to make recommendations for the replacement of English.
(8) "Notwithstanding anything in the aforegoing resolutions, the Federal Legislature may provide for the use, after the expiry of 20 years from the coming into force of the Constitution, of the English language for such purposes as may be specified by law."

The East Bengal Riots

Serious riots occurred in East Bengal during March 1954.

The disorders started in the industrial centres of Chittagong, Narayanganj (near Dacca) and Khulna as the results of the provincial elections became known, and were followed on March 30 by a serious riot at the Government-owned Karnaphuli paper mills at Chandragona, which resulted from a dispute between Bengalis and non-Bengalis and in which three of the executives of the mill and 13 other people were killed.

In Dacca on May 6 a mob stormed the gaol, causing many casualties, while the most serious disturbances occurred on May 14-15, also through a clash between Bengali and non-Bengali workmen, at the Adamji jute mills at Narayanganj, which employed 18,000 men and were the largest in the world. The riots on May 15 actually took place in the presence of Mr. Fazlul Huq, the Chief Minister, and the East Bengal Minister of Labour, Mr. Azizul Huq, who had gone to the factory in an attempt to reconcile the two groups after a fight the previous evening, but while Mr. Azizul Huq was talking with the workmen the fighting began again and went on for several hours. During the riots the labour quarters of the mill were set on fire and over 400 people, including many women and children, were killed and over 1,000 injured before order was eventually restored by troops and police.

During the last week of May Mr. Fazlul Huq and members of his Ministry held a series of conferences with the Central Government in Karachi, at which, in addition to the situation in East Bengal, constitutional and other issues were discussed. In a joint statement issued before leaving Karachi, Mr. Fazlul Huq and his Cabinet colleagues declared: "We want to make it clear once and for all that we are true Pakistanis and stand for the unity and strength of Pakistan. . . . East Pakistan and West Pakistan are integral parts of one component whole, and it is one and indivisible and nothing shall part us. We are for the autonomy of provinces and not for their independence or for separation. . . ."

On May 30 the Governor-General of Pakistan, Mr. Ghulam Mohammed, dismissed the United Front Ministry headed by Mr. Fazlul Huq and introduced Governor's rule under Major-General Iskander Mirza. Mr. Fazlul Huq had shortly before enlarged his

Ministry to 14 members, of whom seven represented the *Krishak Sramik* Party, five the Awami Moslem League and two the *Nizam-i-Islam*.

In a broadcast the same evening Mr. Mohammed Ali denied that the Central Government had been "influenced in the slightest degree by the fact that the Provincial Ministry was not a Moslem League Ministry but a United Front Ministry". He alleged that there were "disruptive forces and enemy agents actively at work in East Bengal to undermine the integrity of Pakistan" and claimed that Mr. Fazlul Huq and his colleagues were not prepared to take the action necessary to cope with the situation.

On his return to Dacca Mr. Fazlul Huq summoned a meeting of his Ministry, which adopted a resolution condemning the Central Government's "arbitrary undemocratic and unconstitutional action", appealing to the public to "maintain peace and tranquillity", and giving an assurance that "all legitimate and constitutional measures will be taken to vindicate the democratic rights of the people". Later on May 31 Mr. Fazlul Huq was placed under armed guard at his home, and Sheikh Mujibur Rahman, Minister for Co-operation in his Government and general secretary of the Awami Moslem League, was put under arrest.

Mr. Huq, who was 84, announced his retirement the following July.

Sind

A political crisis arose in November 1951 from allegations of corruption and maladministration brought against the Chief Minister of Sind, Mr. M. A. Khuhro (who had been dismissed on similar charges in April 1948, but had returned to office in March 1951 after having been cleared by the courts), and three of his four colleagues in the Provincial Cabinet. Mr. Khuhro resisted a demand for his resignation made by the Governor on Dec. 7, but resigned on Dec. 19, together with the Home Minister, after the Governor had informed them that if they did not resign within 24 hours to stand their trial before a special judicial tribunal they would be dismissed. The Minister of Public Works had resigned the previous day. On Dec. 29 the Governor of Sind was asked to take over the provincial administration, as the formation of a stable Ministry in the province had been rendered impossible by "constant strife" among Ministers and in the Moslem League Assembly Party, and to dissolve the Sind Legislature and hold new general elections as soon as conditions permitted.

In view of the repeal of PRODA by the Constituent Assembly [see page 29], and in spite of the qualifications inserted in the repealing Act, the Governor-General, in response to a petition by Mr. Khuhro, issued an Order on Oct. 21 withdrawing with immediate effect the Orders previously made under that Act against Mr. Khuhro.

Provincial elections which took place in Sind on May 9, 1953, resulted in a sweeping victory for the Moslem League, and a new Sind Ministry headed by Pirzada Abdus Sattar, Minister of Food in the former Pakistan Government of Mr. Nazimuddin, was sworn in on May 22, thus ending the Governor's rule in the province which had lasted for 17 months.

West Punjab

Similar action had been taken in West Punjab in January 1949 when the Governor, Sir Francis Mudie, dissolved the Provincial Legislature and assumed charge of the Administration, pending the holding of elections. The Premier of West Punjab, Khan Iftikhar Hussain (the Khan of Mamdot), tendered his Cabinet's resignation on Jan. 25. A government communiqué gave the main cause of the situation as "the failure of the members of the Assembly . . . to rise to the greater responsibility which independence brings".

The Working Committee of the West Punjab Provincial Moslem League adopted on May 22 a resolution demanding the immediate recall of the Governor and his replacement by a Pakistani. Sir Francis Mudie subsequently resigned on July 20, and was replaced by Sardar Abdur Rab Nishtar, the Minister of Communications in the Pakistan Government.

III. MINORITY PROBLEMS AND BORDER DISPUTES, 1948-1959

TALKS ON MINORITIES, 1948

The persistent migration of Hindus from East Bengal (Pakistan) to West Bengal (India), which had been taking place with recurrent intensification since the partition of the province [see page 7], reached its peak during September and October 1948, causing considerable tension between India and Pakistan. Estimates of the numbers involved in the movement varied, the West Bengal authorities claiming that 1,250,000 refugees had arrived between September 1947 and the end of 1948, though the Government of East Bengal characterized these figures as "fantastic".

A solution to the problem of minorities was sought at conferences held in 1948 in Calcutta and New Delhi.

In Calcutta, the Governments of India and Pakistan agreed on April 18 that they would:

(1) seek to discourage the mass exodus of minorities, and to facilitate as far as possible the return of evacuees to their former homes; (2) take all measures to protect the lives and property of minorities, and to safeguard their civic rights; (3) ensure no discrimination on grounds of religion; (4) discourage "any propaganda for the amalgamation of Pakistan and India, or of East and West Bengal, or of Assam and Cooch Behar"; (5) investigate, and promptly remedy, any complaint by minorities of discriminatory treatment; (6) ensure

the setting up of a Minority Board, both in East and West Bengal, consisting of members of both communities and charged with protecting the interests of minorities; (7) take steps to remedy any discriminatory treatment of minorities in matters of trade and commerce; (8) inflict punishment in case of any infringement of the agreement.

The agreement also provided that the East and West Bengal Governments would set up in each province an Evacuees' Property Managing Board, consisting of members of minority communities, to manage property left behind by evacuees, with the specific proviso that these Boards would have no powers to alienate properties administered by them.

In New Delhi, the two Governments agreed on Dec. 14 on further measures implementing the Calcutta Agreement, as follows:

(1) An inter-Dominion Information Consultative Committee would be established to review the communications media, with a view to preventing hostile propaganda and tendentious reports.
(2) The Minority Boards provided for in the Calcutta Agreement would be set up by Feb. 15, 1949 [see above].
(3) A higher judicial tribunal would be established by Jan. 31, 1949, to resolve boundary disputes.
(4) Each Dominion would, by Jan. 1, 1949, simultaneously release government officials of the other against whom criminal proceedings had been taken in respect of matters arising from the execution of their duties (an agreement for the exchange of prisoners and *détenus* guilty of offences before Aug. 1, 1948, had already been reached on Aug. 23, 1948).

Arrangements were made to: (*a*) facilitate travel between both Dominions; (*b*) remove all obstacles to the supply of the commodities provided for in the Karachi Agreement of May 26, 1948; (*c*) permit firms with headquarters in India and Pakistan to send supplies to their branches in the other Dominion; (*d*) safeguard the interests of insurance companies and of their shareholders; (*e*) set up a committee to finalize the division of railway stores (a large measure of agreement was subsquently reached by this committee in Karachi on Dec. 20–22); and (*f*) provide for the payment by Pakistan to India for its share of the defence stores and installations acquired from the U.K. Government.

Partly as a result of these agreements, migration from East Bengal was in mid-January 1949 reported to have almost ceased, and some evacuees had even returned to their homes.

FURTHER AGREEMENT ON MINORITIES, APRIL 1950

Following widespread communal rioting in districts of West Bengal —especially in Calcutta—and in Dacca, Mr. Nehru and Mr. Liaquat Ali Khan (the Indian and Pakistani Prime Ministers), after discussions in New Delhi on April 2–8, 1950, concluded an agreement stating *inter alia:*

"The Governments of India and Pakistan solemnly agree that each shall ensure to the minorities throughout its territory complete equality of citizenship, irrespective of religion, a full sense of security in respect of life, culture, property and personal honour, freedom of movement within each country, and freedom of occupation, speech and worship, subject to law and morality. Members of the minorities shall have equal opportunity with members of the majority community to participate in the public life of their country, to hold political or other office, and to serve in their country's civil and armed forces. Both Governments declare these rights to be fundamental, and undertake to enforce them effectively. . . ."

Minorities from disturbed areas were assured freedom of movement and protection in transit, and undisturbed rights of ownership over property during absence for a limited period. The two Governments would continue their efforts to restore normal conditions and would set up three Minority Commissions to supervise the implementation of the agreement.

Mr. Nehru visited Karachi from April 26–28 for further conversations with Mr. Liaquat Ali Khan covering the whole field of Indo-Pakistani relations. A communiqué issued at the end of the talks on April 27 stated that the two Prime Ministers were satisfied with the progress made in the implementation of the Delhi Agreement; that they had discussed the problems of Kashmir [see pages 45–51], evacuee property, and canal waters [see pages 52–58] "in general terms"; and that they had agreed to continue to hold regular meetings.

Mr. Nehru, in a speech to the Indian Parliament on Aug. 1, 1950, gave the following figures for migrations between East Pakistan and West Bengal, Assam and Tripura (excluding foot travellers):

(*a*) Total number of migrants from East Pakistan to India before and after the Delhi Agreement, 2,142,202 Hindus and 304,255 Moslems;

(*b*) total number of migrants from India to East Pakistan during the same period, 828,746 Moslems and 606,824 Hindus.

About 250,000 Moslems had migrated from Uttar Pradesh (the United Provinces) to West Pakistan; of these 5,000 had returned, and arrangements for the return of others were under consideration.

KARACHI TALKS ON INDO-PAKISTANI DIFFERENCES

Mr. Nehru visited Karachi from July 25–26, 1954, for discussions with Mr. Mohammed Ali, the Pakistan Prime Minister, on problems between the two countries. A joint communiqué issued at the conclusion of the talks on July 27 described them as "frank and cordial", and stated that the subjects discussed had included Kashmir, the canal waters, evacuee and trust properties, Sikh shrines in Pakistan, problems between East Pakistan and West Bengal, Pakistani enclaves in Cooch-Behar and Cooch-Behar enclaves in East Pakistan. The major part of the meeting had been devoted to a discussion of the Kashmir problem and was reported to have "prepared the ground for further talks". In detailed discussions with Pakistan Government officials it had been agreed that the Cooch-Behar enclaves should be exchanged, and that restrictions on travel and trade between the two countries should also be examined, in order that they might as far as possible be removed or minimized. "The Prime Ministers are agreed," the statement concluded, "that the independence and integrity of the two countries must be fully respected, each country having full freedom to follow the policy of its choice in domestic as well as in international affairs. At the same time the Prime Ministers are convinced that the interests of both countries demand the largest possible measure of co-operation between them."

HINDU MINORITIES IN PAKISTAN

Mr. Jogendra Nath Mandal, Minister for Law and Labour in the Pakistan Government since the inception of the Dominion, and the only Hindu member of the Cabinet, resigned on Oct. 8, 1954, on the grounds of dissatisfaction with the treatment of the Hindu minorities in Pakistan, especially in East Bengal. In a letter to Mr. Liaquat Ali, the text of which was issued on the same day, Mr. Mandal wrote that

"Pakistan is no place for Hindus to live in, and their future is darkened by the ominous shadow of conversion or liquidation. . . . Those Hindus who continue to stay in that province, and for that matter in Pakistan, will . . . by stages and in a planned manner be either converted to Islam or completely exterminated." Turning to the "present conditions of and prospects for the Hindus of East Bengal as a result of the Delhi Agreement", Mr. Mandal expressed the opinion that "their condition is not only unsatisfactory but absolutely helpless".

INCREASED MIGRATION BETWEEN INDIA AND PAKISTAN

A sharp increase in migration from East Pakistan to India occurred during the six months September 1954–February 1955, about 65,000 people crossing the border during the last four months of 1954 (an increase of 300 per cent over the figure for the previous four months). Mr. Nehru said in the *Lok Sabha* on March 24, 1955, that deteriorating economic conditions in East Pakistan were an important factor in causing the migration; this was, however, denied by the Pakistani authorities, who attributed the sudden migration to a Press note issued by the West Bengal Government which defined a refugee eligible for rehabilitation as a person who had entered India between June 1, 1947, and Dec. 31, 1954, because of communal disturbances or the fear of such disturbances; this was said to have led many members of this community to cross the border before the final date in the hope of receiving large rehabilitation grants. The continuation of large-scale migration during the first months of 1955, however, was taken in India as an indication that economic conditions in East Pakistan, including a fall in the price of rice, were responsible.

The Pakistani authorities reported at the end of March that there had also been an increase in recent months in the number of Indian Moslems entering West Pakistan through Sind, which had risen to an average of over 2,000 a week.

BOUNDARY DISPUTES

The Judicial Tribunal set up under the Indo-Pakistani agreement of Dec. 14, 1948 [see page 38], to resolve boundary disputes between East and West Bengal and between East Bengal and Assam, held hearings at Calcutta from Dec. 5–16, 1949, and at Dacca from Jan. 4–26, 1950, under the chairmanship of Justice Bagge (Sweden). The Tribunal's report, published on Feb. 5, 1950, settled the disputes as follows:

(1) India's contention in favour of a fixed frontier between the Murshidabad district of West Bengal and the Rajshahi district of East Bengal, rather than one varying with the course of the Ganges, was accepted, the boundary being defined as the midstream of the Ganges as it was on Aug. 15, 1947.

(2) Pakistan's contention that the Mathabhanga River should form the frontier between East and West Bengal over a disputed area of five to ten square miles was accepted by the chairman.

(3) The Tribunal unanimously declared untenable the claims of both India and Pakistan to additional territory in the Patharia Hills Reserve Forest (on the East Bengal-Assam frontier), recommending a continuation of the *status quo* under the Radcliffe award [see page 9].

(4) The Tribunal rejected Pakistan's claim to the town of Karimgunj and the adjacent area on the East Bengal-Assam frontier.

The report proposed that Indian and Pakistani experts should demarcate the boundary lines within one year from Feb. 5, 1950, and that no unilateral action should be taken in the interim by either side.

A conference was held in Calcutta from Sept. 30 to Oct. 3, 1953, to discuss questions at issue between East Pakistan and the Indian States of West Bengal and Assam, and resulted in a settlement of two boundary disputes between East and West Bengal arising from disagreements on the interpretation of the Bagge Tribunal's award.

In 1956 a series of incidents occurred along the Indo-Pakistani borders, for which each side accused the other of responsibility. Subsequently, the Prime Minister of Pakistan announced in the National Assembly on March 19 that he had proposed to the Indian Government the setting-up of a joint boundary commission and the signing of a declaration repudiating war as a means of settling disputes between the two countries. The "no-war" proposal was welcomed by Mr. Nehru the following day.

In a Note of April 9, the Pakistan Government alleged that Indian troops were being concentrated along the West Pakistan border, and demanded their immediate withdrawal to their peacetime stations. The Indian Deputy Foreign Minister completely denied this allegation on April 10. The Indian Government subsequently accused Pakistan of concentrating troops near the Husseiniwala headworks, and in a second Note alleged that Pakistani aircraft had repeatedly flown over the Punjab during the past three weeks. These allegations were in turn denied by the Pakistan Foreign Ministry.

It was announced on April 12 that preliminary work on the demarcation of the borders would begin immediately, starting with the boundary between the Punjab and West Pakistan. The borders of India and West Pakistan (excluding Kashmir) were 1,503 miles long, of which 779 miles had not so far been demarcated by boundary posts, and those of India and East Pakistan 2,463 miles long, of which about 1,500 miles had not been demarcated.

BORDER INCIDENTS

A series of incidents on the frontiers of India and East Pakistan, together with an incident on the Punjab-West Pakistan border in which several Indian policemen were killed, led to a period of renewed tension between the two countries in the spring of 1958 and again in August.

Following an exchange of correspondence between Mr. Nehru and Mr. Noon (the Indian and Pakistan Prime Ministers), a cease-fire came into effect on the border between the two countries from midday on Aug. 26.

Subsequently, a meeting was held between the two Prime Ministers in Delhi on Sept. 9, 1958, and agreements were reached on certain of the disputes, as follows:

(1) The territories covered by the Bagge Award on the West Bengal-East Pakistan frontier [see above], where demarcation had already been completed, would be exchanged by Jan. 15, 1959.

(2) Four other disputes concerning the West Bengal-East Pakistan frontier were considered, in two of which a compromise settlement was reached, while in the other two Pakistan abandoned her claims.

(3) The dispute over the Surma and Piyain rivers would be decided by adopting the latest pre-partition boundary notifications. Whatever the demarcation adopted, full capacities of navigation on these rivers would be given to both sides. In another dispute concerning the Assam-East Pakistan frontier Pakistan abandoned her claim.

(4) On the Tripura-East Pakistan border, India agreed to give

Pakistan a small area of Tripura through which the East Bengal railway passes.

(5) The enclaves of the former Cooch-Behar State in East Pakistan and the Pakistani enclaves in West Bengal would be exchanged without compensation. [The Cooch-Behar enclaves originated as the result of a truce signed after a war between the Moghul Empire and the kingdom of Cooch-Behar, whereby each retained the territories then held by its armies. When the British took over the Moghul Empire the *status quo* remained in force, the former Moghul enclaves inside Cooch-Behar becoming British. In the partition of 1947 these fell under the control of Pakistan. There were 95 Pakistani enclaves inside West Bengal, with an area of 18.3 square miles and a population of 11,000, and 129 Indian enclaves in East Pakistan, with an area of 26.8 square miles and a population of 12,600, the majority of the population in both cases being Moslems.]

Under the agreement, Pakistan would receive about 28 square miles of territory, with a population of about 11,000, in return for about 17 square miles, with a population of about 9,000 which would go to India. The decision to make such an exchange was taken in principle in 1953, but was never put into effect, as no agreement was reached on how West Bengal should be compensated for the extra territory to be transferred to Pakistan.

The Constitution (Ninth Amendment) Bill, which provided for the transfer to Pakistan of the areas specified in the 1958 agreement, was passed on Dec. 20, 1961, and on the same day the Acquired Territories Merger Bill, ratifying the transfer of the areas ceded to India by Pakistan, was passed without opposition.

Following the conclusion of the 1958 agreement no serious incidents occurred on the frontier of Assam and East Pakistan for about two months. Thereafter, however, many incidents were reported between November 1958 and July 1959, and cease-fire agreements concluded by both sides had a temporary effect only.

IV. THE KASHMIR AND CANAL WATERS DISPUTES

THE KASHMIR PROBLEM

During October 1947 a tense situation arose between India and Pakistan over the position of Kashmir State, which at the time of the transfer of power on Aug. 15 had acceded to neither Dominion. The tension was caused early in the month as a result of a number of incidents and alleged "infiltrations" on the frontiers of Pakistan and Kashmir, leading to charges and counter-charges by the Pakistan and Kashmiri Governments against each other.

The situation worsened after an attempted invasion of Kashmir by tribesmen allegedly operating from Pakistan. Indian troops were despatched to restore law and order, and on Oct. 27 it was officially announced that Kashmir had acceded to India. The next day the Indian Prime Minister, Mr. Nehru, informed Mr. Attlee (the British Prime Minister) that he had invited the Pakistan Government's co-operation in stopping raiders entering Kashmir from Pakistani territory; that India's action in Kashmir had been forced upon her by circumstances and by the "imminent grave danger" to Srinagar (the capital of Kashmir); and that India had no desire to intervene in Kashmiri affairs once the State had been cleared of raiders and law and order established. However, a press communiqué issued in Lahore on Oct. 30 stated that "in the opinion of the Pakistan Government the accession of Kashmir to India is based on fraud and violence and as such cannot be recognized".

During 1947 the Indian Union forces in Kashmir, supported by the Royal Indian Air Force, were in operation against the tribesmen from time to time in a number of areas. By the end of the year the tribesmen's advance towards Srinagar had been effectively halted, and by the end of 1948 Indian forces were in control of the greater part of Kashmir.

After the Indian Government had announced in December 1947 that it would place its dispute with Pakistan before the U.N. Security Council, the latter considered the question between Jan. 15 and April 2, 1948, when it adopted a resolution, against Pakistan's objections and with the Soviet Union and the Ukraine abstaining.

The resolution provided for the withdrawal of Pakistani forces from Kashmir; for a progressive reduction of Indian forces, once cease-fire arrangements were effective, to the minimum required "for the support of the civil power in the maintenance of law and order"; and for the holding of a plebiscite to determine Kashmir's future.

A three-member U.N. Kashmir Commission set up on Jan. 17, 1948, was subsequently, on April 24 of that year, increased to five members (Argentina, Belgium, Colombia, Czechoslovakia and the U.S.A.) charged with investigating the situation at first hand.

Mr. Nehru declared to the Indian Parliament on Aug. 20, 1948, that he had evidence that "considerable numbers" of Pakistani troops had been in Kashmir for some months, and that they were stationed both in western Kashmir and in the mountainous regions of the north and north-west. He added that India had protested to Pakistan at the presence of the latter's troops in Kashmir, and that recent operations against Indian positions had been conducted mainly by Pakistani forces. Earlier, a Lahore newspaper had stated that Pakistani troops were aiding the "*Azad* Kashmir" forces (i.e. of the so-called Government of Free Kashmir, set up by the tribesmen under Sheikh Mohammed Ibrahim), adding that the Pakistan Government had decided to send troops to Kashmir the previous May but that their activities had been restricted to "keeping the Indian armies away from the Pakistan border".

The five-nation Kashmir Commission, in a report to the Security Council, stressed that India regarded the presence of Pakistan troops in Kashmir as an act of aggression and insisted on their withdrawal before final negotiations on a truce and cease-fire could begin; and that Pakistan, on its part, demanded the withdrawal of Indian forces and asked that negotiations should include talks with the "*Azad* Kashmir" Government.

Although attempts by the Kashmir Commission to secure a cease-fire and truce had proved unsuccessful, a cease-fire mutually ordered by the Governments of India and Pakistan came into effect at midnight on Dec. 31, 1948, in anticipation of proposals by the Kashmir Commission for the holding of a plebiscite.

The Commission, after meetings with representatives of the Indian and Pakistan Governments, announced on March 12 that agreement in principle had been reached on the definition of a permanent truce line in Kashmir to replace the existing cease-fire line. The main points at issue between the two countries regarding the implementation of the truce agreement were: the disarming and disbanding of the "*Azad* Kashmir" forces; the nature of the "local authorities" who would be responsible for the maintenance of law and order during the plebiscite; and the demarcation of the truce line in northern Kashmir.

A further point of contention in the Kashmir problem was the agreement between Pakistan and China on "the boundary between Sinkiang and the contiguous areas of Kashmir, the defence of which is under the actual control of Pakistan", which was signed in Peking on March 2, 1953. India protested strongly against the agreement, maintaining that the Sino-Pakistani border agreement was illegal, that Pakistan had no authority to surrender any part of Indian territory to China, and that any agreement to that effect was without validity. A protest was lodged with the Security Council later in March.

During discussions between Mr. Mohammed Ali and Mr. Nehru in August 1953, it was decided to appoint a Plebiscite Administrator for Kashmir by 1954. However, in spite of the prospect of a plebiscite, Mr. Nehru stated in the *Lok Sabha* in March 1956 that talk of a plebiscite was "entirely beside the point" and that none could be considered until Pakistan had withdrawn all her armed forces from the State, in accordance with the Security Council's resolution of 1948. This statement, and a subsequent one in which Mr. Nehru intimated that he was no longer in favour of a plebiscite, gave rise to an embittered controversy between the two Governments, culminating

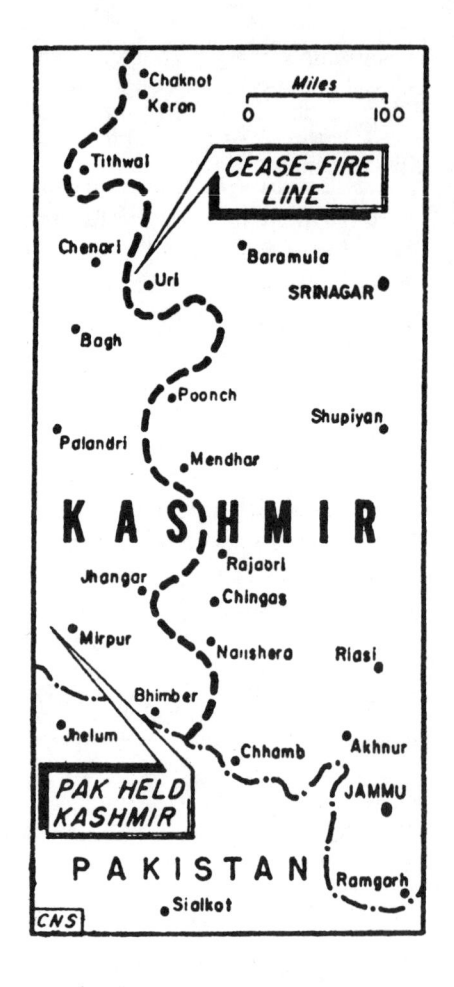

The Cease-fire Line in Kashmir.
(*The Hindu*, Madras)

in Pakistan's decision to refer the Kashmir question back to the U.N. Security Council.

A "Plebiscite Front" was formed in August 1955 by seven members of the Legislative Assembly and a Kashmiri member of the Indian Parliament to campaign for a free and impartial plebiscite under U.N. auspices, the withdrawal of Indian and Pakistani forces from Kashmir, the restoration of civil liberties, and free elections. A number of other Opposition groups subsequently announced their support for this programme. The Kashmir Government, however, took immediate counteraction, all public meetings and processions being banned in Srinagar to prevent clashes between Government and Opposition supporters, and a number of Plebiscite Front spokesmen being arrested for activities prejudicial to the security of the State.

An agreement was finally reached on the proposed true line [see map] on July 26, 1949, and was ratified by the two Governments on July 30.

Five-point Peace Plan

Following protests by India in July 1951 against alleged violations of the cease-fire agreement by Pakistani forces, and allegations by Pakistan of Indian troop concentrations on the Kashmir frontier, the then Pakistan Prime Minister, Mr. Liaquat Ali Khan, put forward a five-point peace plan, the main proposals being:

(1) That all troops should be withdrawn immediately to their normal peace-time stations; (2) that as soon as this had been done India and Pakistan should reaffirm their agreement that Kashmir's accession to either Dominion would be decided by a plebiscite held under U.N. auspices; (3) that both Governments should declare their renunciation of the use of force in the settlement of other disputes; (4) that both Governments should reaffirm the obligation undertaken by them in the Delhi Agreement of April 8, 1950 [see page 39]; and (5) that both Governments should make a declaration that they would not attack or invade the territory of the other.

A prolonged correspondence with Mr. Nehru ensued, but no agreement was reached on the acceptance of the peace plan.

The Constitution

When Kashmir acceded to India in 1947, India took over control of foreign affairs, defence and communications only. In 1954, as a result of further discussions, it was agreed that the Constitution (Application to Jammu and Kashmir) Order of 1950 should be replaced by a more comprehensive Order applying to Kashmir practically all those provisions of the Constitution relating to legislation reserved to India.

President Prasad of India therefore issued an Order on May 14, 1954, extending the application of the Indian Constitution to Kashmir, with the concurrence of the State Government and the Kashmir Constituent Assembly.

The working Committee of the Kashmir National Conference (the ruling party) adopted on Nov. 1, 1954, a resolution declaring that "limited accession to India is our final and irrevocable decision", and rejecting the alternatives of accession to Pakistan or complete independence.

A draft Constitution for Kashmir, declaring the State to be "an integral part of the Union of India", was presented to the Kashmir Constituent Assembly on Oct. 10, 1956, and came into force on Jan. 26, 1957 [Indian Independence Day], provisions being made for general elections to be held as soon as possible. The Constitution declared *inter alia* that all sovereignty rested with the State, which had executive and legislative powers in all matters "except those in respect of which Parliament [i.e. the Indian Parliament] has power to make laws for the State under the provisions of the Constitution of India".

The Prime Minister of Pakistan repudiated the validity of the Constitution in a statement on Nov. 17 in which he said that "Pakistan has not recognized and will never recognize the right of this [the Constituent Assembly] or any other such body to represent and legislate on behalf of the people of Jammu and Kashmir State".

Jan. 26 was observed as a "black day" throughout Pakistan in protest against the integration of Kashmir with India, widespread anti-Indian demonstrations taking place in Karachi, Lahore, Hyderabad (Sind) and Dacca.

The Foreign Minister of Pakistan, Mr. Firoz Khan Noon, requested the president of the U.N. Security Council on Jan. 2, 1957, to convene a meeting of the Council "at a very early date" to resume consideration of the Kashmir question, in view of the forthcoming entry into force of the new Constitution and the integration of Kashmir with India as from that date.

When the Security Council subsequently met in January 1957 to consider the question, Mr. Firoz Khan Noon proposed that all Indian and Pakistani forces should be withdrawn from Kashmir and that a U.N. force should be sent there to enable a plebiscite to be held. Mr. Krishna Menon, the Indian Minister of State, in a reply lasting almost eight hours, maintained that the real issue was the Pakistani invasion of Kashmir, and denied that the introduction of the new Constitution represented any fundamental change in the situation.

During the next few years little progress was made on the Kashmir question. Hr. Gunnar Jarring, the Swedish representative on the U.N. Security Council, visited the subcontinent for discussions in March and April 1957 but failed to initiate any moves towards reconciling Indo-Pakistani differences. Dr. Frank P. Graham, the U.N. representative for India and Pakistan, also visited India and Pakistan in January and February 1958, and in his report, published on April 3, he gave details of a five-point peace plan which he had submitted to the two Governments. The recommendations were accepted by the Pakistan Government in principle, but were rejected by India on the grounds, *inter alia,* that they would "place the aggressor and the aggressed on the same footing".

In December 1963 trouble flared up again in Kashmir after the theft of a relic of the Prophet Mohammed from a mosque, which deeply shocked Kashmiri Moslems, causing the gravest political crisis in the State for several years and leading to serious riots in Srinagar.

Mr. Bhutto, the Pakistan Foreign Minister, alleged on Jan. 1, 1964, that the theft of the relic had been "permitted by the Indian occupation authorities and their puppets as part of India's plan to reduce the Moslem majority in Jammu and Kashmir to a minority, by bringing home to its Moslem population the feeling that the lives, honour and religion of Moslems are not safe, and that therefore they must leave the State".

The unrest in Srinagar, together with an earlier announcement that the State's Constitution would be amended to strengthen its integration with India, accentuated the tension between India and Pakistan over the Kashmir question, and led to an increase in the number of incidents on the cease-fire line.

Further serious incidents in 1965 led to the outbreak of hostilities between India and Pakistan. For details of these events see Chapter VII, pages 88–91.

THE CANAL WATERS DISPUTE

The partition of the Punjab between India and Pakistan in 1947 gave rise to a prolonged dispute between the Governments of the two countries concerning their respective rights over the waters of rivers and canals flowing from India into West Pakistan and used for irrigation purposes by both countries, the bulk of the Punjab irrigation system being left in Pakistan and the headworks of the canals supplying the irrigated areas in India.

A dispute had arisen between the East and West Punjab Governments with regard to the supply by the East Punjab of water from the Ferozepore headworks (in East Punjab) to the Bari-Doab canal in West Punjab, which irrigated some 1,500,000 acres in the Lahore, Lyallpur, and Montgomery areas of Pakistan; whereas the East Punjab Government maintained that proprietary rights in the waters of the East Punjab rivers were vested in itself, and that the West Punjab could not claim any share in those waters as of right, the latter Government contended that, as its economy was completely dependent upon those rivers, it was entitled in international law and equity to an equal share in their waters. In the Indian view the problem was primarily a technical one, and the Indian Government therefore proposed that a joint technical survey of the water resources of the Indus basin should be undertaken, after which outstanding questions could be settled by a judicial tribunal on which both countries were equally represented; the Pakistan Government, on the other hand, insisted on a settlement of the legal issue by means of an appeal to the International Court of Justice as an essential first step. The dispute was intimately connected with that over the future of Kashmir, as three of the six rivers involved (the Indus, Jhelum and Chenab) flow into West Pakistan from or through Kashmir, and in consequence the Pakistan Government claimed that Indian control of Kashmir would put the entire economy of West Pakistan at India's mercy—a view which, however, was denied by India.

Although certain temporary agreements had been signed in 1947 and 1948—e.g. a joint agreement signed on May 4, 1948, providing that East Punjab would continue to supply water to West Punjab for irrigation purposes while giving the latter province sufficient time to develop alternative water resources, and stating that East Punjab had no intention of withholding water supplies suddenly from the latter

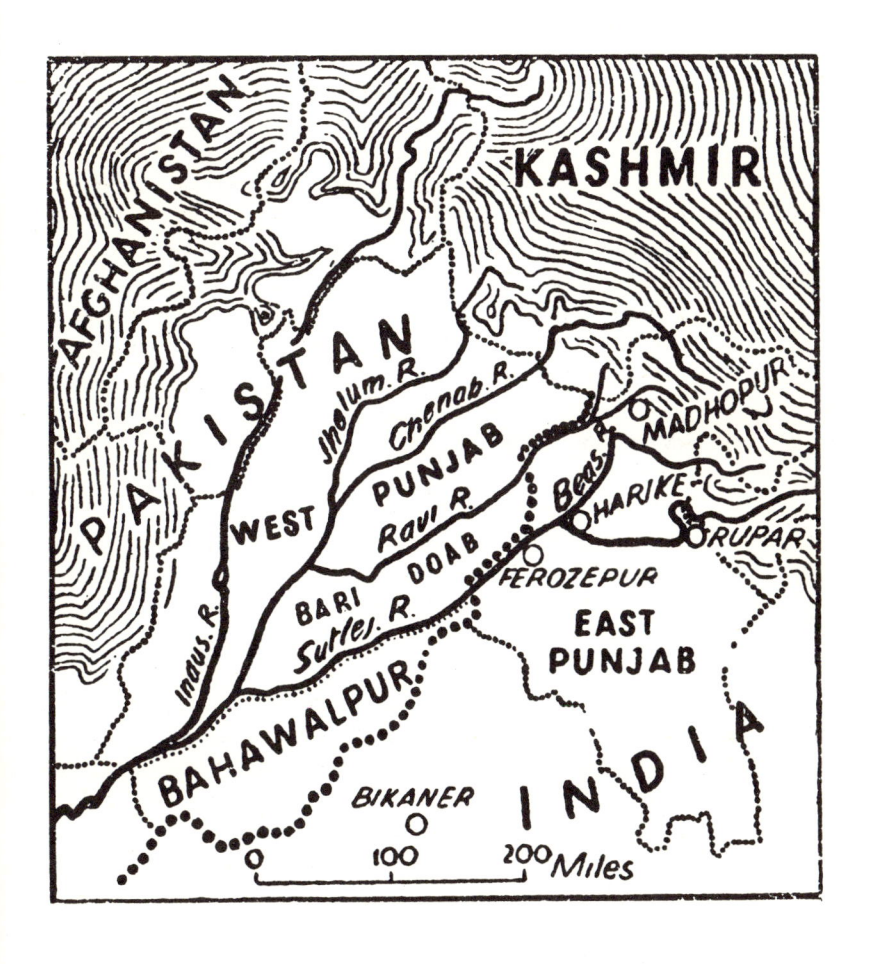

The map shows the six rivers of the Indus Basin—the Indus, Jhelum, Chenab, Ravi Sutlej, and Beas—whose waters form the subject of dispute between India and Pakistan. (*Economist*)

province without giving it time to tap alternative sources—protracted negotiations between India and Pakistan on the canal waters dispute continued at intervals for four years thereafter, between 1948 and 1952, but without any definite result.

Allegations that India had drastically curtailed the supply of water to canals feeding vast tracts of land in West Pakistan were put forward by the Pakistan Government in January and February 1953. The fear was also expressed that India might totally stop supplies of water as some of her own irrigation projects (such as the Bhakra Dam, work on which had commenced before partition, and the Harike canal system) approached completion.

Mr. Nehru expressed surprise at Pakistan's accusation and gave the explanation that there was less water available owing to drought in both East and West Punjab which affected supplies to both areas. Mr. Nehru stressed that India had continued to supply water under the 1948 agreement [see page 52]—which, as far as India was concerned, was still in force—and renewed his offer to refer the matter to a joint tribunal, and points on which the tribunal disagreed to any international authority.

Negotiations were resumed during 1952 on the initiative of Mr. Eugene Black, president of the International Bank for Reconstruction and Development (World Bank), who proposed (during a visit to India and Pakistan in February of that year) that the two Governments should make a joint technical survey of the Indus basin, and who offered any assistance, financial or technical, that the Bank could give in the matter. Mr. Black's suggestion having been accepted by both Governments on the basis that existing uses should be respected, discussions between Indian and Pakistani engineers and representatives of the International Bank took place in New York in May and June 1952. Following the failure of these discussions, the Bank in February 1954 submitted to the two Governments a comprehensive plan of its own for the division of the water resources of the Indus Basin. The main points of the plan were:

(1) The entire flow of the three western rivers of the Indus system (the Indus, Jhelum, and Chenab) would be available for the exclusive use of Pakistan, except for a small volume of water for Kashmir.

(2) The entire flow of the three eastern rivers (the Ravi, Beas, and Sutlej) would be available for the exclusive use of India, except that for a specified transitional period India would supply to Pakistan "her historic withdrawals from these rivers". This period, estimated at five years, would be worked out on the basis of the time required to complete "link canals" needed in Pakistan to replace these supplies.

(3) Each country would construct and pay for the works located in its territory, but India would also bear the cost of link canals in Pakistan needed to replace supplies from India "to the extent of benefit derived by her therefrom".

Although India accepted these proposals, the Government of Pakistan asked for a delay before it gave its decision, in order to obtain an independent report on the proposals from a United States firm of hydraulic engineers; this report, when it was received, expressed the opinion that the plan was defective and would involve Pakistan in a serious water shortage for irrigation developments already planned. In May the Bank appealed to Pakistan either to accept or reject the proposals within a week, so that India would be free to develop and utilize her own water resources. The Pakistan Government, however, proposed a detailed technical study before Pakistan finally accepted or rejected the scheme. The Indian Government informed the Bank on June 21 that it regarded Pakistan's reply as tantamount to a rejection, and it therefore regarded as void the agreement of March 13, 1952, i.e. the suggestion of the president of the International Bank, Mr. Eugene Black, that "so long as co-operative work continues with the participation of the Bank, neither side will take any action to diminish [water] supplies available to the other side for existing uses".

The Indian Government nevertheless expressed its willingness to consider new arrangements for working out a comprehensive plan on the basis of the Bank's proposals as soon as Pakistan agreed to accept them, and also to enter into an agreement for a transitional period which would enable developments to proceed in both countries on an agreed schedule, as envisaged in the Bank's proposals.

Pakistan "conditionally" accepted the Bank's proposals on Aug. 5, 1954, as a basis for a resumption of negotiations, subject to certain clarifications.

Mr. Nehru opened the Bhakra canal system on July 8, 1954, thereby releasing the waters of the Sutlej River into the canal. Pakistan protested strongly, alleging that the canal presented a threat to its water supplies and food production. A spokesman for the International Bank, however, stated that the opening of the Bhakra canal, which had been anticipated and taken into consideration in the discussions, did not, in the Bank's view, present any new problem at the moment, as for the next two months the flow of water would be sufficient for Pakistan's needs. In September, however, the supply to Pakistan might be affected, and this point was under discussion between representatives of the Bank, India, and Pakistan.

Mr. Mohammed Ali announced on Aug. 5 that Pakistan had "conditionally" accepted the Bank's proposals, adding that his Government would "try the World Bank formula, accept it if it is workable, and guarantee proper usage of the waters". On the same day the Bank informed the Indian Embassy in Washington that Pakistan was prepared to accept the proposals, subject to certain clarifications, as a basis for a resumption of negotiations. The Indian Government, in reply, expressed its willingness to discuss conditions with a view to evolving a clear basis for a new working party with the participation of the Bank, and discussions were resumed on Dec. 6, 1954. On June 21, 1958, temporary agreement on the use of the waters of the Indus basin for irrigation purposes was reached after a mission from the Bank had visited Pakistan and India in March and April and had toured the areas concerned with Pakistani and Indian engineers and officials.

The agreement was later extended, and subsequently further agreements were signed covering 1956 and 1957; however, negotiations for a new agreement to replace that which had expired in March 1957 broke down, and a new interim agreement was signed only in April 1959 after further prolonged negotiations under the auspices of the International Bank.

THE INDUS WATERS TREATY

A treaty governing the use of the waters of the Indus system of rivers, and ending the critical and long-standing dispute between India and Pakistan, was signed in Karachi on Sept. 19 by Mr. Nehru, President Ayub Khan, and Mr. W. A. B. Iliff, Vice-President of the International Bank for Reconstruction and Development.

The drafting of the Treaty had begun in August 1959 and entailed further negotiations, under the auspices of the World Bank, directed towards securing agreement on the many complicated technical and financial details which had to be specifically incorporated in any final document.

The Treaty in Outline

"The Preamble to the Treaty recognizes the need for 'fixing and delimiting in the spirit of goodwill and friendship the rights and obligations' of the Government of India and the Government of Pakistan concerning the use of the waters of the Indus River System.

"The Treaty allocates the waters of the three Eastern Rivers—Ravi, Beas, and Sutlej—to India, with certain exceptions specified in the Treaty. The main exception is that during a Transition Period, while the works are being constructed in Pakistan for the replacement of Eastern River water, India will continue to deliver water to Pakistan from the Eastern Rivers in accordance with a schedule set out in an annexe to the Treaty. The Transition Period will be ten years, but may in certain circumstances be extended by a further one, two, or three years.

"The waters of the three Western Rivers—Indus, Jhelum, and Chenab—are for the use of Pakistan, and India undertakes to let flow for unrestricted use by Pakistan all the waters of these three rivers, subject to Treaty provisions that some of these waters may be used by India in areas upstream of the Pakistan border for the development of irrigation, electric power, and certain other uses spelled out in detail in annexes to the Treaty.

"Pakistan undertakes to construct, during the Transition Period, a system of works, part of which will replace, from the Western Rivers, those irrigation uses in Pakistan which have hitherto been met from the Eastern Rivers. . . .

"Both countries recognize their common interest in the optimum development of the rivers, and declare their intention to co-operate by mutual agreement to the fullest possible extent. . . ."

The Indus Works Programme

"The division of waters provided for in the Treaty necessitates the construction of works to transfer water from the three Western Rivers to meet the irrigation uses in Pakistan hitherto met by water from the three Eastern Rivers. The effect of the transfer will be eventually to release the whole flow of the three Eastern Rivers for irrigation development in India. The system of canals and reservoirs that will actually be constructed will, however, provide further substantial irrigation development, and will develop important hydro-electric potential, in both India and Pakistan. It will also make a much-needed contribution to soil reclamation and drainage in Pakistan, and provides a measure of flood protection in both countries.

"The programme will be the largest of its kind to be undertaken anywhere."

Under an Indus Basin Development Fund Agreement, the Fund (administered by the World Bank) was provided with sources of foreign exchange. The United States and the World Bank also provided considerable loans.

Further details published in Delhi showed that the division of the total waters of the Indus system under the Treaty was in the proportion of 80 per cent for Pakistan and 20 per cent for India. The latter country guaranteed to let flow for all time to come the waters of the Indus, Jhelum, and Chenab Rivers to Pakistan, except for essential uses in its territory specifically laid down in the Treaty.

V. THE CONSTITUTION OF 1956—POLITICAL DEVELOPMENTS, 1956-1957—ABROGATION OF CONSTITUTION, 1958

ELECTION OF NEW CONSTITUENT ASSEMBLY

In May 1955 the constitutional crisis which had arisen from the dissolution of the Constituent Assembly in October 1954 [see page 30] was finally resolved.

The Sind Chief Court in February 1955 declared illegal the Governor-General's proclamation which had dissolved the Constituent Assembly, and ruled moreover that five members of the Central Government who were not members of the Assembly were not entitled to exercise their ministerial offices. The Government appealed against this decision, and hearings began before the Federal Court of Pakistan at the beginning of March. The Court subsequently announced on March 21 that it accepted the Government's appeal against the Sind Court's decision, and also ruled that the Governor-General's assent was necessary to all legislation passed by the Central Legislature. The consequence of this ruling was that 44 Acts which had not received the Governor-General's assent became invalid, e.g. as the Constituent Assembly had changed its composition in 1950 by laws which did not receive the Governor-General's assent, it could be maintained that it had become an illegal body and that all Acts subsequently passed by it were invalid; similarly, an Act which had extended the Governor-General's powers to pass constitutional enactments by ordinance became invalid, as did all ordinances enacted during that period.

In view of the situation, the Governor-General on March 27 issued an Emergency Powers Ordinance which, *inter alia*, legalized retrospectively 35 of the 44 Acts invalidated by the Federal Court's decision, and empowered him to take all necessary steps for the purpose of framing a Constitution. On April 12, however, the Federal Court ruled that only the Constituent Assembly could draw up a Constitution for Pakistan, and that the Governor-General had no authority to revalidate constitutional measures rendered void by lack of his assent, or make a Constitution by ordinance.

In conformity with this, Mr. Ghulam Mohammad issued an Order summoning a Constituent Convention to meet on May 10 in order to validate the measures in dispute and to draw up a Constitution for Pakistan.

In order to "avoid a possible breakdown in the constitutional and administrative machinery of the country" during the interim period pending the meeting of the Constituent Convention, Mr. Ghulam Mohammed issued a proclamation on April 10 arrogating to himself the necessary powers to validate such invalid laws as were needed to preserve the State and to maintain the rule of law. At the same time he validated retrospectively the 35 laws mentioned in the Emergency Powers Ordinance [see above] and all Orders made under those laws, subject to a report of the Federal Court and until such time as the Constituent Convention enacted appropriate new legislation. Mr. Ghulam Mohammed also asked the Federal Court for an interim Order restraining all courts—until the Federal Court's report was received—from taking any action on the ground that any law mentioned in the schedule to the Emergency Powers Ordinance was invalid.

The Federal Court granted this Order on the same day, but suggested that the Governor-General should also refer to it for advice on the question of the legality of the dissolution of the Constituent Assembly and on the competence of the proposed Convention to exercise its powers. On May 10 the Court ruled that the Governor-General had legal authority to dissolve the Assembly, to summon a new Assembly, and to validate laws retrospectively during the interim period before it met, but not to nominate members to the new Assembly.

Mr. Ghulam Mohammed, in a message to the nation which was

broadcast on May 10 by the Prime Minister, Mr. Mohammed Ali, stated that the Federal Court's decision had cleared the way for the setting-up of a new Constituent Assembly, which would be convened "within the shortest possible time".

In the elections to the new Pakistan Constituent Assembly, which were held on June 21, 1955, no one party secured a majority, the results being as follows: Moslem League 25, United Front 16, Awami League 13, Independents 4 (including 2 non–Moslem members), Pakistan National Congress 4, Scheduled Castes Federation 3, "Noon group" 3, United Progressive Parliamentary Party 2, *Azad* Pakistan Party 1, Communists 1. The Assembly met for the first time on July 7.

THE CONSTITUTION OF THE ISLAMIC REPUBLIC OF PAKISTAN

The Pakistan Constituent Assembly adopted on Feb. 29, 1956, the Constitution Bill, under which Pakistan became an Islamic Republic, and on March 2 decided that Pakistan should remain within the British Commonwealth.

The Constitution, which consisted of 234 Articles, was divided into 13 parts, of which Part I dealt with the Republic and its territories, Part II with fundamental rights, Part III with directive principles of State policy, Part IV with the Federation, Part V with the provinces, Part VI with the relations between the Federation and the provinces, Part VII with property, contracts, and suits, Part VIII with elections, Part IX with the judiciary, and Part X with the Services of Pakistan. Part XI dealt with emergency provisions, Part XII with general provisions, and Part XIII with temporary and transitional provisions. There were also six Schedules, the first of which dealt with the election of the President, the second with oaths and affirmations, the third with the powers of the Supreme Court and the remuneration of judges, the fourth with the remuneration and privileges of the President, the Speaker and Deputy Speaker of the National Assembly and the Provincial Assemblies, members of the National Assembly and the Provincial Assemblies, and Provincial Governors; the fifth with the lists of subjects for which either the Federation or the provinces, or both concurrently, would be competent to legislate; and the sixth with the election of the first President of the Republic.

The main provisions of the Constitution, which was published in draft form on Jan. 8 and underwent considerable revision in the Assembly, are summarized below.

The Republic and its Territories. Article 1 stated that "Pakistan shall be a Federal Republic, to be known as the Islamic Republic of Pakistan", its territories comprising (*a*) the provinces of East Pakistan and West Pakistan, (*b*) the States which had already acceded or might accede to Pakistan, (*c*) federally administered territories not included in either East or West Pakistan, and (*d*) such other territories as might be included in Pakistan.

It was also laid down that the President might, by Order, make provision for the government and administration of the territories specified under (*b*), (*c*) and (*d*) until otherwise provided for by legislation.

Fundamental Rights. All citizens would be equal before the law, and no person might be deprived of life or liberty save in accordance with the law.

The independence of the judiciary was guaranteed.

The President. The President of the Republic, who must be over 40 years of age and a Moslem, would be elected for a five-year term by an electoral college consisting of members of the Central and Provincial Legislatures. He would have supreme command of the armed forces, would be empowered to dissolve the National Assembly upon the Prime Minister's advice, and would appoint the Election Commission and the Public Service Commission. No person might serve as President for more than two terms.

The Cabinet. The President would, "in his discretion", appoint from amongst the members of the National Assembly a Prime Minister who, in his opinion, was "most likely to command" the confidence of a majority of the Assembly members. Other Ministers, Ministers of State and Deputy Ministers would be appointed and removed from office by the President, but only members of the National Assembly could become Ministers of State or Deputy Ministers.

The National Assembly. The National Assembly would consist of 300 members equally divided between West and East Pakistan, and would be elected for five years on a basis of adult suffrage. For the first 10 years additional seats in the National Assembly would be reserved for women—five elected by women's territorial contituencies in West Pakistan and five by similar constituencies in East Pakistan.

Legislative and Special Powers of the President. When a Bill had been passed by the National Assembly, the President could within 90 days either (*a*) assent to the Bill; (*b*) withhold his assent; or (*c*) —in the case of a Bill other than a money Bill—return it to the Assembly with the request that the Bill, or any provision thereof, should be reconsidered, and any amendment specified by him be taken into consideration. If in cases (*b*) and (*c*) the Assembly again passed the Bill, with or without amendment, by a two-thirds majority of the members present and voting, the President must assent to the legislation (Article 57).

Article 69 provided: "If at any time, except when the National Assembly is in session, the President is satisfied that circumstances exist which render immediate action necessary, he may make and promulgate such Ordinances as the circumstances appear to him to require, and any Ordinance so made shall have the like force of law as an Act of Parliament." Any Ordinance made by him under this clause might, however, be controlled or superseded by an Act of Parliament.

The Provinces. Each province would have a Governor who would be appointed or dismissed by the President. Each province would have a Cabinet of Ministers, headed by a Chief Minister, whose functions and responsibility to the Provincial Assembly would correspond to those of the Federal Government to the National Assembly.

Each Provincial Assembly would have 300 members plus another 10 seats reserved for women members for a 10-year period.

Division of Powers. The Central Government would protect the provinces against external aggression. The allocation of responsibilities between the Central and Provincial Governments would conform to the policy of provincial autonomy, whilst vesting in the Central Government responsibility for matters of national interest.

Emergency Provisions. "If the President is satisfied that a grave emergency exists in which the security or economic life of Pakistan, or any part thereof, is threatened by war or external aggression, or by internal disturbance beyond the power of a Provincial Government to control, he may issue a Proclamation of emergency. . . ." (Article 191, Section 1).

Amendment of the Constitution. The Constitution might be amended by an Act of Parliament passed by a majority of the Assembly's membership and a two-thirds majority of members present and voting. The amendment of Articles dealing with the territories of the Federation, the composition of the National Assembly and Provincial Assemblies, the division of legislative competence between the Federation and the provinces, and the composition and functions of the National Economic Council and the National Finance Commission, would also require the consent of the Provincial Assemblies before the President could give his assent.

The draft Constitution, as published, represented a compromise between the two Government parties—the Moslem League and the United Front. The recognition of Bengali as an official language, and the establishment of a National Economic Council, had been demanded by the United Front, which, in return for these concessions, had abandoned its demand for full provincial autonomy and the limitation of the Centre's powers to the spheres of defence, foreign affairs and currency. No agreement was reached at this stage, however, on the question of joint electorates [see pages 66–67]. The clauses declaring Pakistan an Islamic Republic and excluding non-Moslems from the office of President encountered strong opposition from the Pakistan Congress and the United Progressive Party (two Hindu organizations supporting the United Front). The East Pakistan Awami League criticized the powers granted to the President, and demanded full regional autonomy for the provinces.

The draft Constitution was submitted to the Constituent Assembly on Jan. 9, 1956.

THE UNIFIED PROVINCE OF WEST PAKISTAN

Under an Order issued on Oct. 5, 1955, by Major-General Iskander Mirza, then Acting Governor-General of Pakistan, the unified Province of West Pakistan came into being on Oct. 14. Under the Establishment of West Pakistan Bill, which had been given a third reading in the Constituent Assembly on Sept. 30, the following were integrated into the new Province: the former provinces of Sind, Punjab and North-West Frontier Province; the city of Karachi; the former States of Baluchistan, Bahawalpur and Khairpur; the former Frontier States and Baluchistan States Union; and the former Frontier Province Tribal Areas. West Pakistan was divided into 10 divisions, which were subdivided into 50 districts under deputy commissioners.

The integration of the provinces of West Pakistan had first been announced in November 1954 when Mr. Mohammed Ali announced in a broadcast that the Government had decided to merge the existing four provinces and 10 Princely States of West Pakistan into a single administrative unit, and to make the country a Federation of two units—West Pakistan and East Pakistan (hitherto East Bengal). West

Pakistan, as a single unit, would have a population of 34,000,000, and East Pakistan of 44,000,000. The integration would enable the Government to conserve its administrative and economic resources and to devote them more effectively to the rapid development of the two provinces of East and West Pakistan, thereby making the administration both considerably cheaper and vastly more efficient. With West Pakistan as a single political unit, the task of framing the new Constitution would be very much simplified.

Consequently, a number of political changes had been made during November 1954 in Sind, Bahawalpur and Khairpur aimed at furthering the unification of West Pakistan.

In Sind, the Governor dismissed Pirzada Abdus Sattar's Ministry on Nov. 8 on the grounds of "maladministration" and appointed Mr. M. A. Khuhro as Chief Minister. Pirzada Abdus Sattar himself said that his dismissal was due to his stand in the Constituent Assembly against the merging of the West Pakistan provinces into a single unit, and claimed that his view reflected the "unanimous will" of the people of Sind against the One-Unit proposal.

In Bahawalpur the Amir dismissed the State Ministry on Nov. 2, dissolved the State Legislature and entrusted the administration to an adviser appointed by the Central Government. Major-General Mirza stated that the Amir had acted with the Central Government's approval, and that the Ministry had been dismissed because of "maladministration".

In Khairpur the State Assembly unanimously adopted a resolution on Nov. 10 favouring the merger of the State in a single unit embracing the whole of West Pakistan.

The Government's proposals were subsequently endorsed by the various Provincial Assemblies and were generally welcomed throughout West Pakistan, although some opposition was expressed in Sind and Karachi, where student demonstrations took place. Resolutions approving the scheme were adopted by the Legislative Assembly of the North-West Frontier Province unanimously on Nov. 25, 1954; by the Punjab Legislative Assembly by a large majority on Nov. 30; by the Sind Legislative Assembly on Dec. 11; and by the *Shahi Jirga* of Baluchistan on Nov. 29. The Khan of Kalat expressed his support on Nov. 23, and it was announced on Jan. 3, 1955, that an agreement had been signed by the Khan and the other Rulers of the States forming the Baluchistan States Union for the merger of all these States (Kalat, Makran, Las Bela and Kharan) in a unified West Pakistan.

Closely connected with the question of establishing West Pakistan as One Unit was the decision to give both provinces parity of representation, first in the Constituent Assembly and then in the National Assembly. Such an arrangement was incorporated in the Constitution of 1956, and although this arrangement aroused growing dissatisfaction in East Pakistan because of its larger population, which in the interest of balancing the two Wings was deprived of the full weight of its voting strength, and despite persistent criticism of the One-Unit system in West Pakistan, both the latter and the parity of representation in the National Assembly were retained in the new Constitution of March 1962 [see page 79]. The membership of the National Assembly was, however, cut to 150 plus six seats reserved for women, again equally divided between East and West Pakistan.

THE ELECTORATE BILL

In drafting the Constitution, no agreement could be reached on the question of whether Moslems and non-Moslems should form a single electorate, or whether the minorities should return separate representatives in national and provincial elections. The majority of the United Front, the East Pakistan Awami League and the Hindu community were in favour of joint electorates, whereas this view was opposed by the Moslem League and also by the *Nizam-i-Islam,* one of the constituent parties of the United Front. It was therefore laid down that the National Assembly should reach a final decision after taking into consideration these views.

The deep division of opinion on this issue subjected the Central Government to severe strain. The secretary-general of the Republican Party (which together with the Awami League made up the Government coalition) declared on Sept. 28, 1956, that the party was committed to separate electorates in both provincial and national elections, and was prepared to co-operate even with the Moslem League against the Awami League on this issue. As the Awami League—which drew its main support from East Pakistan—had consistently supported joint electorates, a Cabinet crisis was averted only by the decision, adopted at a meeting of Government supporters in the National Assembly on Oct. 9, to accept a compromise. On Oct. 10 the Government's Electorate Bill was introduced, providing that elections to both the National and Provincial Assemblies should be held on the basis of a joint electorate in East Pakistan (where 25 per cent of the population were non-Moslems) and separate electorates in West Pakistan (where non-Moslems formed a much smaller minority). The Bill was passed on Oct. 12, the Republicans and the Awami League voting in favour and the Moslem League and the United Front opposing.

During April 1957 the National Assembly considered several Bills relating to the preparation of general elections throughout the country in March 1958, the most important of these measures being the Electorate Amendment Bill, which introduced a system of joint electorates for both West and East Pakistan, and thus amended the Electorate Act.

The Electoral Rolls Bill, which was passed on April 30, regulated the qualifications of voters at national and provincial elections and the preparation of electoral rolls. Its object was to clear the way for the Election Commission to make the necessary preparations for the first general elections in the country on the basis of universal adult franchise.

The Representation of the People Bill regulated the membership of the National Assembly and the two Provincial Assemblies; laid down the qualifications and disqualifications for membership; defined corrupt and illegal practices and other offences in connexion with elections; and regulated the procedure for decisions on election disputes. It laid down that the National Assembly would comprise 310 members, half of whom would be elected by West Pakistan and the other half by East Pakistan, and that the two Provincial Assemblies would also have 310 members each.

The Bill was referred to a Select Committee.

POLITICAL DEVELOPMENTS IN PAKISTAN, 1956–1957

West Pakistan

Following the election in January of the new Interim Legislative Assembly of West Pakistan, as laid down in the Establishment of

West Pakistan Bill, the Moslem League Assembly Party decided on April 3, 1956, to withdraw its support from Dr. Khan Sahib on the ground that the Chief Minister should be a member of the League. Dr. Khan Sahib, however, succeeded in forming a new Cabinet to replace the Moslem League Ministers who had resigned, and formed his own party, the Republican Party, which received the support of a large number of former Moslem League members, thus ensuring it a majority in the Assembly. The party would operate as a separate group inside the Assembly, but would continue to support Chaudhri Mohammad Ali's Government.

After Dr. Khan Sahib's Ministry had lost its majority in the Provincial Assembly in March 1957 on the issue of the breaking up of West Pakistan into autonomous provinces, President Mirza suspended the Constitution on March 21. Mr. Abdur Rashid Khan (the Minister of Finance) took over the leadership of the Republican Party and the post of Chief Minister until March 1958, when he resigned both offices after the National Awami Party had withdrawn its support for the Republicans in favour of the Opposition Moslem League, while five Republican members of the Assembly also joined the Moslem League. The reason for the National Awami Party's move was that it had entered into an agreement with the Moslem League for the joint formation of a coalition Government in West Pakistan on the basis of a 16-point programme (which, however, was confined to agrarian and administrative problems).

East Pakistan

In East Pakistan, severe floods in August 1955 led to a serious rice shortage and resulted in a food crisis. The Government was widely criticized for its handling of the situation, and a constitutional deadlock arose out of the Speaker's refusal to allow the presentation of the Budget estimates. President Mirza accordingly suspended the Constitution on May 26, 1956, and authorized Government expenditure for three months before revoking his proclamation on June 1.

On Aug. 9, 1956, the Governor of East Pakistan, Mr. Fazlul Huq, announced that the Provincial Assembly, which had been prorogued since May 22, would meet on Aug. 13 to discuss the Budget. In preparation for the new session, seven motions of no-confidence in Mr. Abu Hussain Sarkar's United Front Government were submitted by the Opposition parties, in addition to motions condemning the Government's food policy and the detention of members of the Assembly under the East Bengal Public Safety Act. [Mr. Fazlul Huq had previously amended the Assembly's rules of procedure by increasing from 99 to 130 the number of members whose support was needed before the Assembly could consider a no-confidence motion.]

Four hours before the Assembly was due to meet, it was prorogued by Mr. Fazlul Huq on Mr. Sarkar's advice. Talks on the situation opened on Aug. 18 between President Mirza and Chaudhri Mohammad Ali (then Prime Minister) on the one hand, and Mr. Fazlul Huq and Mr. Sarkar on the other.

The United Front Parliamentary Party, after discussions lasting three days, decided on Aug. 29 to advise Mr. Sarkar's Ministry to resign; it also adopted a resolution endorsing Mr. Sarkar's advice to the Governor to prorogue the Assembly. Mr. Sarkar consequently submitted his resignation on Aug. 30, and on the following day President Mirza provisionally suspended the Constitution in the province and on Sept. 6, for the second time within just over three months, proclaimed President's rule.

A new Cabinet, formed by Mr. Ataur Rahman Khan, leader of the East Pakistan Awami League, took office on Sept. 6.

An open split in the Awami League occurred during the first half of 1957 owing to sharp dissensions between Mr. Hussein Shaheed Suhrawardy, the Prime Minister and all-Pakistan Convener of the League, and Maulana Bashani, its president in East Pakistan. The points at issue were the Maulana's demand for full regional autonomy for East Pakistan in internal matters and for a policy of "neutrality and independence" in foreign affairs, including Pakistan's withdrawal from the Baghdad Pact and SEATO and the rejection of foreign economic aid. A new party—the National Awami Party—was subsequently formed with the Maulana as president.

A serious crisis occurred on March 31, 1958, when Mr. Ataur Rahman Khan requested the Governor to prorogue the Provincial Assembly because the Cabinet had obtained a majority of only 15 votes in a debate on the Budget estimates—a request which Mr. Huq refused. Mr. Huq subsequently dismissed the Ministry of Mr. Khan (Mr. Sarkar immediately taking over as Chief Minister), but was then himself dismissed later the same night by President Mirza, the Chief Secretary of West Pakistan, Mr. Hamid Ali, being appointed Acting Governor. Within 12 hours of Mr. Khan's dismissal by Mr. Fazlul Huq, Mr. Sarkar, in turn, was dismissed by Mr. Hamid Ali, who reinstated Mr. Khan and his entire Cabinet.

When the Provincial Assembly (which had been adjourned on April 5) reassembled on June 12 a fresh crisis broke out, the National Awami Party ordering its 30 members in the Assembly "not to lend any further support" to the Awami League coalition ministry headed by Mr. Khan unless the League was willing to sign the National Awami Party's five-point programme. Mr. Khan was accordingly defeated in the Assembly on June 19 by 138 votes to 126, the National Awami members abstaining. On the following day Mr. Sarkar (*Krishak Sramik* party) was sworn in as Chief Minister, but shortly before the swearing-in ceremony the Awami League and the National Awami Party announced that they had concluded a coalition agreement, and later the same day both parties decided to move a no-confidence motion against Mr. Sarkar, which was adopted.

In view of the situation Governor's rule was imposed in East Pakistan and the Provincial Assembly prorogued for a period of two months. On the expiring of this period Mr. Ataur Rahman Khan was commissioned to form a new Ministry.

When the Provincial Assembly met again on Sept. 20, 1958, a Moslem League member protested against the presence of six Government supporters who had been disqualified by the Election Commission. [The Commission had ruled that the office of public prosecutor, which all these members held, was an office of profit; although a Bill was subsequently passed by the National Assembly making the holding of this office no longer a disqualification, it was not given retrospective effect and an Ordinance had to be issued by the President for this purpose.] The Speaker, Mr. Abdul Hakim, reserved his ruling on this question, ruled out of order a motion of no-confidence in himself proposed by Government supporters, and named several Awami League members for disorderly conduct. A fight then broke out; Government and Opposition members attacked one another with chairs and steel microphone stands, the national flag was torn down and trampled on, and Mr. Hakim, who narrowly escaped serious injury, was forced to leave the Chamber.

On Sept. 21-22 the Assembly had to be adjourned as both sides had introduced hundreds of their supporters into the lobbies. On Sept. 23 the police excluded all outsiders from the premises, and also prevented Mr. Hakim from entering the Chamber. When Mr. Shahed Ali, the Deputy Speaker, tried to take the chair Opposition members pelted him with pieces of furniture, causing such serious injuries that he died two days later; the police then entered the Chamber and forcibly expelled the Opposition, two of whom were injured and taken to hospital. Several Opposition members, including Mr. Sarkar, were arrested on Sept. 24 and charged with the attempted murder of Mr. Ali, but were released on bail. The Provincial budget was passed on the same day in the absence of the Opposition, who were boycotting the House, and the Assembly was then adjourned.

With the President's proclamation of Oct. 7 [see below] the Provincial Governments and Assemblies were dissolved.

CABINET CRISIS AND ABROGATION OF CONSTITUTION

In order to widen the basis of his Government, Mr. Firoz Khan Noon, the Prime Minister, had discussions during September 1958 with Mr. Suhrawardy and Mr. Hamidul Huq Choudhury, the respective leaders of the Awami League and the *Krishak Sramik* party which belonged to the coalition supporting Mr. Noon's Cabinet. As a result, the Cabinet was enlarged and portfolios were reallocated. Mr. Choudhury was sworn in as a Minister on Sept. 16, and acted as Finance Minister during the absence of Syed Amjad Ali in Canada. Although Mr. Suhrawardy refused to join the Government himself, three members of the Awami League took office as Ministers and three others as Ministers of State. Two Republicans had previously been sworn in as Ministers of State on Sept. 20. These changes increased the size of the Government to 17 Ministers and nine Ministers of State (eight Ministers and four Ministers of State from West Pakistan, and nine Ministers and five Ministers of State from East Pakistan), out of a National Assembly of 80 members.

The reallocation of portfolios in the enlarged Cabinet gave rise to intense controversy. On returning to Karachi, Syed Amjad Ali refused to relinquish the Finance Ministry in Mr. Choudhury's favour, and threatened to leave the Republican Party with 10 other deputies, including a number of Ministers.

On Oct. 7 Mr. Noon announced a Cabinet reshuffle, whereby he himself relinquished the Foreign Ministry to Sardar Abdur Rashid (formerly Minister of Commerce and Industries); Syed Amjad Ali retained the Finance Ministry, and Mr. Choudhury became Minister of Commerce.

Immediately these appointments were made known, the Awami League decided to recall its six representatives in the Government as a protest against the allocation of portfolios; it stated that Mr. Noon was facing grave difficulties inside the Republican Party over the distribution of portfolios between East and West Pakistan, and that these difficulties were "of such a nature that the very purpose of the Awami League's entry into the Cabinet—to ensure the holding of free and fair elections on the appointed date of Feb. 15—may be thwarted". Mr. Noon subsequently reshuffled his Cabinet a second time to exclude the Awami League representatives.

On Oct. 7, 1958, a few hours after the crisis inside the Cabinet, President Mirza issued a proclamation in which he abrogated the Constitution, dismissed the Central and Provincial Governments, dissolved the National and Provincial Assemblies, abolished all political parties, proclaimed martial law, and appointed General Ayub Khan (C.-in-C. of the Army) as Chief Martial Law Administrator. Both the wording of the proclamation and subsequent statements by President Mirza and General Ayub made it clear that the President's action, in which he was fully supported by the Army, was motivated by his conviction that the political parties were responsible for the "chaotic internal situation" and would "rig the elections for their own ends". Recent developments which apparently brought matters to a head included—in addition to party disputes over posts in the Central Government—the riotous scenes in the East Pakistan Assembly between Sept. 20–23 [see pages 70–71] and violent agitation by the Moslem League, whose paramilitary organization was suppressed by the Government on Sept. 20.

On Oct. 24, President Mirza appointed General Ayub Khan as Prime Minister and formed a new Cabinet consisting entirely of non-political personalities. It was stated that the new Government was a Cabinet "in the accepted sense of the term", indicating its joint responsibility though it had no parliamentary basis.

President Mirza on Oct. 28 relinquished his office of President to General Ayub Khan.

IRAN
AFGHANISTAN
Kabul
Khyber Pass
Islamabad
Kandahar
Rawalpindi
Lahore
PAKISTAN
Delhi
New Delhi
NEPAL
Kathmandu
Indus R.
Karachi
Rann of Kutch
Jumna R.
INDIA
Gange
Narmada R.
Cal
ARABIAN SEA
Bombay
Godavari R.
Hyderabad
Madras
CEYLON
Colombo

THE INDIAN and INDOCHINESE PENINSULAS

VI. CONSTITUTIONAL DEVELOPMENTS UNDER AYUB KHAN, 1959–1962

THE BASIC DEMOCRACIES SYSTEM

President Ayub Khan said at a press conference on Dec. 2, 1958, that once the Government had solved such vital problems as the resettlement of refugees, land reforms and modification of the educational and legal systems, it would "consult the best brains and ascertain the feelings of the people in order to draw up a Constitution suited to the needs of our country". Pakistan would not copy any other country's Constitution, but would have one entirely of its own, in keeping with the country's social and economic condition. He himself favoured the presidential system of government, whereby a President was elected either by universal suffrage or through electoral colleges, but once the President was elected he must be given fairly wide powers to run the country's affairs. The parliamentary system, he added, could be worked only if politicians strictly followed the spirit of the Constitution and the electorate was educated enough to force its representatives to do the right thing.

It was accordingly decided in 1959 to create a four-tier structure of "Basic Democracies"—popular bodies comprising men who represented the people and were in close touch with them, and which were to assist the authorities in rural development, social welfare and national reconstruction. A Basic Democracies Order was promulgated by President Ayub Khan on Oct. 26, 1959, under which councils were to be constituted as follows:

(1) A Union *panchayat* (Village Council) for a union in rural areas, and a Town Committee for a town, or a Union Committee for a union, in urban areas.

(2) A *Thana* Council for each *thana* (sub-district) in East Pakistan, and a *Tehsil* Council for each *tehsil* in West Pakistan.

(3) District Councils.

(4) Divisional Councils.

These would form the four tiers, and there would in addition be two Provincial Development Advisory Councils for East Pakistan and West Pakistan (these were constituted in May 1960).

The Order also laid down details of electoral procedure, taxation, development plans, and police and defence functions.

Elections to the "Basic Democracy" units were held in East and West Pakistan between Dec. 26, 1959, and Jan. 9, 1960. The delimitation of constituencies had been finalized during November, and the martial law regulations which prohibited the organization, convening or attending of any political meeting or procession had been amended by President Ayub Khan on Dec. 1 to allow meetings organized by candidates for the forthcoming elections. The number of primary units whose membership was to be elected totalled about 4,000 in West Pakistan and over 4,000 in East Pakistan, while the seats to be filled numbered about 80,000.

Before the announcement of the election results, the Cabinet resolved that a secret ballot on a vote of confidence in President Ayub Khan should be held by the 80,000 members elected to the Basic Democracy councils. The resolution added: "If the majority of votes cast is in the affirmative, it should be treated as a mandate for the President to take the necessary steps forthwith for setting up constitutional machinery in Pakistan, and he should also be deemed to have been elected President of Pakistan for the first term of office under the Constitution to be so made."

According to the official results of the ballot, which was held on Feb. 14, 1960, the President received 75,283 affirmative votes, or 95.6 per cent of the votes cast. He was sworn in as President on Feb. 17, and immediately afterward announced the setting up of a Constitution Commission.

The aims of the Constitution Commission were (*a*) to examine the "progressive failure of parliamentary government in Pakistan leading to the abrogation of the Constitution of 1956, and to recommend how a recurrence of similar causes can be prevented"; and (*b*) to submit proposals for a Constitution which would embody recommendations on how best to achieve: a democracy "adaptable to changed circumstances and based on the Islamic principles of justice, equality and tolerance"; the consolidation of national unity; and a firm and stable system of government.

A Law Reform Commission and an Education Commission were also appointed, and on Nov. 10, 1958, it was announced that all troops employed in the enforcement of martial law in West Pakistan had been withdrawn, except in the Karachi area, and that all military courts had been dissolved. Similar announcements were made in East Pakistan on the following day.

Despite President Ayub Khan's statement on Nov. 17 that he had never intended the armed forces to replace the civil administration, and that martial law would from then on be the responsibility of the civil authorities, new regulations were promulgated by the President on Feb. 28, 1959, giving military courts sole jurisdiction in offences against martial law and authorizing the re-establishment of summary and special military courts throughout the country. It was stated that this measure was designed to strengthen the authorities' fight against black-marketeering and crime.

On Dec. 28, 1961, far-reaching changes were announced in the administration of West Pakistan, designed to delegate financial, executive and administrative powers to regional, divisional and district officers and thus to decentralize the administrative organization. The Government's decision was based on the recommendations of the Provincial Reorganization Committee, which had been set up in February 1959.

In addition to accepting the Committee's recommendations, the Cabinet also decided that Divisional Councils as well as the councils at lower levels would be entrusted with final authority in certain administrative matters hitherto dealt with only by officials, thereby actively associating the Basic Democracies with the maintenance of law and order; and that a drastic budgetary reform would be carried out, not only in West Pakistan as recommended by the Committee but also in East Pakistan and the Centre.

THE NEW CONSTITUTION OF 1962

The new Constitution of the Second Republic of Pakistan, setting up a presidential system of government, was announced by President Ayub Khan on March 1, 1962. The Constitution was based on a report of the Constitution Commission, which had been presented to the President in May 1961.

Announcing the new Constitution, President Ayub Khan described it as a "blending of democracy with discipline—the two prerequisites to running a free society with stable government and sound administration". He outlined its "salient features" as follows:

(1) The country would be called the Republic of Pakistan.
(2) The new Constitution was federal in character and provided for a presidential form of government, with a unicameral Legislature at the Centre and also in each of the two provinces.
(3) All executive authority would vest in the President.
(4) Dacca would be the principal seat of the Central Legislature, while Islamabad would be the principal seat of the Central Government.
(5) Urdu and Bengali would be the two national languages of Pakistan.
(6) There would be parity in the Central Legislature, which would have 150 members. In addition six seats would be reserved for women, three from each province.
(7) Each province would have maximum autonomy; thus the residuary powers would be vested in the Provincial Legislatures.
(8) A convention would be established whereby, when the President was from West Pakistan, the Speaker of the National Assembly would be from East Pakistan, and *vice versa*.
(9) During the absence of the President, the Speaker of the National Assembly would officiate in his place.
(10) All Pakistani citizens would be equal before the law.
(11) All legitimate interests of minorities, including their religious and cultural interests, would be fully safeguarded. "Untouchability" would be forbidden.
(12) The Constitution guaranteed all citizens: (*a*) freedom of speech, (*b*) freedom of association, (*c*) freedom of employment and the right to acquire property.
(13) The President would have power to appoint Ministers from among persons qualified to be elected to the National Assembly.
(14) The Constitution could be amended by a two-thirds majority of the National Assembly and with the concurrence of the President.

If the President did not concur, a three-quarters majority of the House could override his veto. In that case, however, the President would have the option of referring the matter to a referendum or of dissolving the Assembly. In the latter case he must himself seek re-election within 120 days of the dissolution.

(15) There would be an "Advisory Council of Islamic Ideology", consisting not only of the *Ulemas* but also of eminent research scholars and experts in many fields of the nation's activities. The Council's function would be the maintenance of the Islamic spiritual and moral values side by side with the country's material progress.

A reorganization of the Central Government machinery was announced on April 26, 1962, providing for 11 Ministries and five Divisions in the President's Secretariat. The 11 Ministries would be: Defence; External Affairs; Finance; Commerce; Home and Kashmir Affairs; Industries and Natural Resources; Communications; Health, Labour, and Social Welfare; Education and Information; Law and Parliamentary Affairs; and Agriculture and Works, including Rehabilitation.

The President's Secretariat would consist of the following Divisions —Cabinet; Planning; Establishment; Economic Affairs; and States and Frontier Regions.

REVIVAL OF POLITICAL PARTIES

President Ayub Khan issued an Order on May 10, 1962, banning the revival of organizations for political purposes until the National Assembly had had time to examine the whole question of political parties "after full and public discussion", and to legislate upon it. The Order prohibited the setting-up of political organizations, as well as the collection of funds for them, and the acquisition or ownership of property by such organizations. It also provided that no association of persons, with or without an organizational structure, could call itself by any of the former party names.

When the new National Assembly met for the first time on June 8, 1962, President Ayub Khan (who was sworn in during the session as the first President of Pakistan under the new Constitution), addressing the session, stressed that martial law had been lifted with the entry into force of the Constitution and that the country was governed by the normal law of the land.

The principal measures passed by the new Assembly were the Political Parties Bill, legalizing the formation of political parties and their participation in elections, and the Preventive Detention Laws Amendment Bill, providing that no person could be detained for more than three months without the authority of a board consisting of a Supreme Court judge and a senior government official nominated by the President. If the two members differed on the legality of the detention, the detainee would be released. Both Bills were introduced by the Government following strong demands from all sides of the House for the lifting of the continued ban on political parties and for the release of political detainees.

Following the enactment of the Political Parties Bill on July 14, President Ayub Khan held a press conference on July 20 at which he called on "right-minded" Pakistanis to form a broadly-based nationalist political party with a progressive outlook, indicating that he himself might join such a party. However, in place of one broadly-based party, a number of different parties emerged during 1962.

The Moslem League, which had been banned with all other parties, was revived in 1962 and split into three factions, one of which —the "conventionists", who favoured the party's revival on a broad basis—supported President Ayub Khan's Government, while the other two—the "Council group" and the "non-revivalists", who maintained that the party could not be re-established pending the restoration of full democracy—allied with the other Opposition parties in demanding the democratization of the new Constitution.

Two leaders of the former Awami League (Mr. Ataur Rahman Khan and Sheikh Mujibur Rahman) likewise said that the question of a revival of that party did not arise, a similar statement being issued by the leaders for the former *Krishak Sramik* party. Both statements alleged that the political climate in Pakistan was still unsuitable for the working of democratic political organizations.

Meanwhile, the formation had been announced in June of the "Democratic Group", a section of the East Pakistan members of the National Assembly claiming the support of over 40 out of 78 members from East Pakistan. The formation of an Opposition group of East Pakistani members in the National Assembly, under the name of the People's Democratic Group, was announced in August.

In October 1962 the "National Democratic Front" was formed to press for, *inter alia,* the introduction of adult franchise, the justiciability of fundamental rights, and a parliamentary system of government. The Front was supported by the "Council" Moslem League, the Awami League, the National Awami Party, the *Krishak Sramik* party and the *Nizam-i-Islam* party, as well as sections of the Republican Party and the *Jamaat-i-Islami*. A demand that the President should hold a round-table conference with prominent politicians to discuss amendment of the Constitution was rejected by the President on the ground that such a procedure would be unconstitutional.

However, on March 9, 1963, the Constitution Amendment Bill, which recognized the fundamental rights provided for in the 1956 Constitution [see pages 61–63], was introduced in the National Assembly, and was passed on Dec. 25 as the Fundamental Rights Bill. Its provisions were as follows:

(1) The country would be known as the Islamic Republic of Pakistan, and all existing as well as future laws would be brought within the purview of the principle barring legislation repugnant to the Koran and the Sunna.
(2) All fundamental rights enshrined in the Constitution would become "justiciable" or enforceable in the courts, but 31 laws made under the martial law regime would be excepted from any such judicial scrutiny. The exempted laws included the West Pakistan Criminal Law Amendment Act (formerly the Frontier Crime Regulations Act), the Political Parties Act, the Public Offices Disqualification Order of 1959, and the Moslem Family Laws Ordinance of 1961.
(3) The jurisdiction of the High Court and the Supreme Court would not apply to the Tribal Areas.

The National Assembly then passed on June 11, 1964, the Constitution (Second Amendment) Bill, which *inter alia* advanced the presidential election by five months and fixed the life of the electoral college at five years. Opposition members strongly criticized a provision that the President should retain office until his successor was inducted. [The Constitution had previously provided that the President should remain in office for five years and 60 days, and that if elections were not completed by the end of his term the Speaker of the Assembly should assume the Presidency as an interim arrangement.] The Government, however, secured the majority of two-thirds of the entire Assembly (104 votes out of 156) required for the adoption of a constitutional amendment, after nine Opposition members had crossed the floor, the Bill being passed by 106 votes to 26.

In addition to the Constitution Amendment Bill, the National Assembly also approved during 1964 a number of other Government-sponsored measures laying down the legislative framework for the presidential, National Assembly and Provincial Assembly elections. They were:

The Electoral College Bill. This provided for the election by general suffrage of 80,000 electors who in turn would elect the President of the Republic, the National Assembly and the two Provincial Assemblies for respectively East and West Pakistan early in 1965.

The Elections Bill. The National Assembly approved on Aug. 8, 1964, a Bill to provide for the holding of elections to the National and Provincial Assemblies in respectively March and May 1965. The Bill, with a number of Government amendments to meet points raised by the Opposition, was passed without a division.

The Presidential Election Bill. A Bill for the conduct of elections for the office of President, introduced on Aug. 10, 1964, was finally approved on Aug. 18, after Opposition speakers had again vehemently criticized the method of indirect election and urged the election of the President by direct vote on an adult franchise.

Elections to the electoral college took place in October and November 1964. About 75 per cent of the electorate voted in West Pakistan and 90 per cent in East Pakistan. The voting gave rise to widespread disorders in West Pakistan, fighting between the rival parties causing numerous casualties. The Opposition parties accused the ruling "conventionist" Moslem League of organizing large-scale intimidation and impersonation of voters, with the connivance of the police. So great was the tension in Karachi, the principal Opposition stronghold in West Pakistan, that the district magistrate on Nov. 10 banned public meetings and processions for two months. Some disturbances occurred in East Pakistan, where Opposition support was stronger, but they were less serious than those in West Pakistan.

PRESIDENTIAL ELECTIONS

Field Marshal Ayub Khan (who had been nominated by the "conventionist" Moslem League, having become their president in December 1963) was re-elected President of Pakistan for a five-year term on Jan. 2, 1965, defeating his main opponent, Miss Fatima Jinnah, by a majority of almost two to one.

Following the nomination of the candidates, a series of 10 "confrontation meetings" was held in the principal towns from Dec. 8-24, at which the candidates addressed members of the electoral college, outlining their programme and policies and answering questions; although the general public was not admitted to these meetings, the Press was allowed to report them.

Although President Ayub Khan declared that he was willing "to give all possible guarantees that we have every intention to hold the elections on schedule and fairly and squarely", and that he had no intention of perpetuating his rule, the Opposition complained that it had been greatly handicapped during the campaign by the Government's control of the radio, whereas President Ayub made frequent broadcasts and his speeches were reported at length. Opposition spokesmen were refused broadcasting time and Miss Jinnah's speeches received only brief reports. Foreign correspondents reported, however, that she had been given fair coverage in the Press.

Miss Jinnah said on Jan. 3: "There is no doubt that these elections have been rigged. . . . The entire conduct of these elections has been marred by flagrant official interference, police high-handedness, intimidation, corruption and bribery. . . . To claim in these circumstances that these elections were fair and impartial is absolutely untenable. . . ."

In an eve-of-poll broadcast, President Ayub said on Jan. 1, 1965, that the parliamentary form of government, which Miss Jinnah aimed at restoring, had made Pakistan "the laughing-stock of friend and foe". It was essential for Pakistan, with two zones separated by a hostile distance, to have a strong central authority. This did not mean consolidation of power in the hands of a single individual, however; there was, he claimed, more delegation of power to the provinces under the present Constitution than ever before.

President Ayub Khan received 64 per cent of the vote in the country as a whole—74 per cent in West Pakistan, and 53 per cent in East Pakistan.

Following the election, violent rioting, in which at least 20 people were killed and 50 seriously injured, broke out in Karachi on Jan. 4, 1965, after Mr. Guahara Ayub Khan (one of the President's sons) had led a "victory procession" through the city. Lorry-loads of armed Pathan supporters of the Government drove into suburban areas inhabited largely by Moslem refugees from India, most of whom were known to have supported Miss Jinnah, and there assaulted passers-by, looted shops and houses, and set fire to huts, a number of people being burnt to death in their homes.

The President's new term of office began on March 23, 1965—on which date in 1940 the Moslem League had adopted the "Pakistan resolution" envisaging the establishment of an independent Moslem State.

NATIONAL AND PROVINCIAL ASSEMBLY ELECTIONS

Elections for a new National Assembly were held in Pakistan on March 21, 1965, the electoral college consisting of the 80,000 "Basic Democrats" who had themselves been elected in the autumn of 1964 [see page 83]. The final results of the elections were as follows:

Moslem League (conventionist)	126
*Combined Opposition Parties	13
Independent Group	10
Other Independents	6

* These were the parties which supported Miss Fatima Jinnah as their joint presidential candidate, viz. the "Council" Moslem League, the Awami League, the National Awami Party, the *Nizam-i-Islam* and the *Jamaat-i-Islami*.

Elections to the Provincial Assemblies in West and East Pakistan were held in May 16, 1964, the Moslem League taking the lead in both provinces.

VII. INDO-PAKISTANI RELATIONS, 1959–1966

An improvement in the relations between India and Pakistan after a period of estrangement during 1959 (due mainly to border incidents, and to the shooting down in April of an Indian jet bomber which had allegedly violated Pakistani airspace) was marked by discussions on trade and financial questions, and culminated in a brief meeting between President Ayub Khan and Mr. Nehru on Sept. 1—the first meeting between the two leaders since President Ayub Khan's assumption of office in October 1958. As a result of the meeting, discussions took place on Oct. 15–22, 1959, in Delhi on the question of border disputes.

Full agreement was reached, not only on the principal disputes on the India-East Pakistan border, but also on the adoption of "ground rules" governing the conduct of the Army and police forces on both sides, and on principles for provisional demarcation—aimed at preventing any further incidents where demarcation had not yet been reached on any particular dispute. Moreover, it was agreed that all outstanding disputes on the India-East Pakistan and India-West Pakistan borders "should, if not settled by negotiation, be referred to an impartial tribunal", and that both Governments were determined to implement "in full and as expeditiously as possible the Nehru-Noon agreement [see page 43] and the present agreement".

A further conference took place in January 1960, it being announced on Jan. 11 that both sides had reached full agreement on all outstanding disputes over the border between Punjab (India) and West Pakistan, and that the only dispute still to be settled was that relating to the West Pakistan border with Bombay State in the Rann of Kutch.

COMMUNAL DISTURBANCES

During 1961 and 1962 communal disturbances in India had led to similar disturbances in Pakistan: riots in Jabalpur (India) in February 1961 were followed by riots in Karachi and in several areas of East Pakistan, while clashes between Santhals (a tribal people) and Moslems in West Bengal in March and April 1962 were followed by widespread communal disorders in East Pakistan. In June 1962 and during the following months allegations were repeatedly made by the Pakistan Government that Indian Moslems were being forcibly expelled from Assam and Tripura and driven into East Pakistan. These allegations were, however, categorically denied by the Indian Government, which contended that all the Moslems evicted from Assam and Tripura were Pakistani nationals who had entered India illegally, primarily for economic reasons.

The gravest communal disturbances since 1950 occurred in East Pakistan and the eastern States of India during the first three months of 1964, leading to large-scale migration of the minority communities from both countries.

Following the theft of the relic of the Prophet Mohammed from the Hazratbal shrine in Kashmir [see page 51], violent communal rioting broke out on Jan. 3, 1964, in the Khulna and Jessore districts of East Pakistan. The disturbances at Khulna began when a procession of 20,000 demonstrators entered the town, and continued until Jan. 9, Hindus being murdered and their houses looted and set ablaze. As hundreds of Hindu refugees fled into West Bengal to escape the riots, disturbances began in Calcutta and many rural areas of West Bengal, and these were followed by outbreaks of rioting in East Pakistan, about 75,000 non-Moslems crossing the frontier into Assam during the latter half of January and in February.

The concentration of the bulk of the refugees in West Bengal, where 3,400,000 refugees had already settled since 1947, aroused fears that their presence would provoke new communal outbreaks, and it was therefore decided to disperse them. An unforeseen result of this policy was the spread of communal rioting to a large area of southern Bihar, western Orissa and eastern Madhya Pradesh as trainloads of refugees passed through these States.

President Ayub Khan protested against the Calcutta riots which, he alleged, had been encouraged by the Indian Government's policy of evicting Moslems. President Radhakrishnan of India rejected the Pakistan President's allegations; maintained that the disturbances in West Bengal had been caused by those at Khulna; and suggested that they should issue a joint appeal for communal peace to the people of both countries.

A conference was held in Delhi on April 7, 1964, but no agreement was signed, the questions of the eviction of Indian Moslems to East Pakistan and the migration of Hindus from East Pakistan being postponed to the next round of talks.

Following the death of Mr. Nehru on May 27, 1964, President Ayub Khan made a fervent appeal for friendship between Pakistan and India in a broadcast on June 1, in which, having paid tribute to the late Indian statesman, he said that he extended "the warm hand of friendship to the Indian people" and declared that Pakistan would "respond to any sincere move for the improvement of Indo-Pakistani relations". His appeal met with a warm response from Mr. Lal Bahadur Shastri in the latter's first broadcast on June 11 as Prime Minister of India.

INDO-PAKISTANI HOSTILITIES IN RANN OF KUTCH, 1965

The number of clashes on the borders of East Pakistan and the Indian States of Tripura, Assam and West Bengal, which had occurred at intervals since 1962, increased greatly during the first half of 1965. However, the most serious incidents occurred in April 1965 in the Rann of Kutch, on the frontier between the Indian State of Gujarat and West Pakistan, and continued at intervals until the end of the month.

The Rann (desert), which covers an area of about 8,400 square miles, is a vast expanse of tidal mud-flats, flooded during the monsoon season; though uninhabited and of little economic value, Pakistan had included a section of the Rann in the coastline to be surveyed for offshore drilling by an American oil company. The Indian Government claimed that the whole of the Rann formerly belonged to Kutch, and hence became part of India when the State acceded to the Indian Union in 1947. The Pakistan Government, on the other hand, claimed that about 3,500 square miles of the Rann lying north of the 24th parallel were formerly under the control and administration of Sind. It also contended that the Rann was a landlocked sea or boundary lake, and that under international law the boundary must run through the middle of the area; this argument was rejected by India, on the ground that the British Government of India formally decided in 1906 that it was more correct to define the Rann as a marsh rather than as a lake.

Following a clash between Indian troops and Pakistani police in the Rann of Kutch and a series of incidents on the Punjab border, it was agreed in 1956 to demarcate the border between India and West Pakistan. Although agreement was reached on the Punjab-West Pakistan border and the boundary demarcated in 1960, the Kutch-Sind boundary dispute remained undecided, and it was agreed in January 1960 to collect further data and to hold discussions later with a view to reaching a settlement. No such discussions took place, however.

Fighting broke out on April 9, 1965, following allegations of mutual violation of territory, and continued intermittently until a *de facto* cease-fire came into effect at the end of the month. Through the mediation of the British Government a formal cease-fire agreement was signed on June 30, which provided for talks between the two Governments at ministerial level and the reference of their territorial claims to a tribunal if no agreement was reached. At the Indian Government's suggestion the proposed ministerial talks were cancelled on Aug. 18, and it was agreed to refer the question at once to a tribunal.

Following the fighting in the Rann of Kutch, both India and Pakistan concentrated troops near other sectors of their frontiers, but after the conclusion of the cease-fire agreement in the Rann, President Ayub Khan ordered on July 2, 1965, the withdrawal of Pakistani troops from the frontiers, and similar orders were issued to the Indian forces.

THE KASHMIR CRISIS OF 1965—
THE TASHKENT DECLARATION

The number of clashes between the Indian and Pakistani forces on the cease-fire line in Kashmir had greatly increased during 1964, and still more during the first half of 1965. Finally, a serious crisis in Indo-Pakistani relations, resulting in large-scale fighting between their armed forces, was precipitated when on Aug. 5, 1965, armed infiltrators from *Azad* Kashmir began entering Indian Kashmir in an unsuccessful attempt to foment revolt. Further parties of infiltrators entered on Aug. 18, but an Indian protest was rejected by Pakistan.

The number of incidents on the cease-fire line in Kashmir had reached an unprecedented level in May and June, responsibility being attributed by the U.N. to both sides; however, the number declined after the signing of the Rann of Kutch cease-fire agreement [see above]. Exchanges of fire all along the line became increasingly frequent after Aug 8, and on Aug. 16 Indian troops crossed the line and occupied Pakistani posts. In early September Pakistani forces advanced into the Indian sector, capturing a key post on Sept. 5, and on the same day the Indian Defence Ministry announced that Pakistani aircraft had attacked an Indian Air Force ground unit near Amritsar, without causing any damage; the operation was the first reported to have occurred outside Kashmir. On the following day Indian troops, without a declaration of war, launched an offensive across the Punjab frontier into West Pakistan. The Indian Defence Minister claimed that the Indian attack had been launched in order to forestall an attack by Pakistan on Indian Punjab.

In a broadcast on the same day President Ayub Khan declared that "we are at war", and announced that he had proclaimed a state of emergency, although an Indian Government spokesman afterwards stated: "India is not at war with Pakistan or the Pakistani people. India's operations are intended to destroy Pakistan military bases from where they attacked India."

Fighting continued on three fronts until Sept. 23.

The U.N. Security Council adopted early on Sept. 20 a draft resolution which stated *inter alia*:

"The Security Council . . . demands that a cease-fire should take effect on Wednesday, Sept. 22, 1965, at 0700 hours GMT, and calls upon both Governments to issue orders for a cease-fire at that moment and a subsequent withdrawal of all armed personnel back to the positions held by them before Aug. 5, 1965."

At Pakistan's request a special meeting of the Security Council was held in the early hours of Sept. 22, at which Mr. Bhutto announced Pakistan's decision to order a cease-fire, but warned the Council that if it did not bring about a settlement of the Kashmir question within a limited time Pakistan would leave the United Nations.

The cease-fire came into effect as ordered, but was jeopardized from the outset by a series of violations by both sides and by their refusal to withdraw from the positions which they held in each other's territories. The Indian Government alleged that after the cease-fire strong Pakistani forces had intruded into both the Fazilka area and many border areas of Rajasthan which they had not previously occupied, and a number of engagements took place in both sectors.

An emergency meeting of the Security Council on Sept. 27 adopted a resolution demanding that both India and Pakistan "urgently honour their commitments to the council", and calling upon them "promptly to withdraw all armed personnel".

Both sides, however, continued to accuse each other of numerous violations of the cease-fire, particularly in Kashmir and in the Fazilka and Rajasthan sectors.

Mr. Swaran Singh, the Indian Minister of External Affairs, informed U Thant (the U.N. Secretary-General) on Oct. 1 that India would observe the cease-fire unconditionally but not unilaterally, and would retaliate if Pakistan violated it. She would withdraw her forces provided that Pakistan withdrew all hers, including the infiltrators in Kashmir. India, he added, was not prepared to link the cease-fire or withdrawal of forces with any political question, as Kashmir was an integral part of India and therefore "not negotiable".

The President of Pakistan and the Prime Minister of India began discussions on Jan. 4, 1966, in Tashkent (Soviet Union) following the Soviet Government's offer in November 1965 of its good offices in helping to resolve the Indo-Pakistani dispute. The Soviet Prime Minister, Mr. Alexei Kosygin, was in Tashkent throughout the six days' negotiations and played a vital part in their eventual successful termination, after it had seemed at one time that they would end in deadlock. Largely as a result of Mr. Kosygin's mediatory efforts, the talks ended on Jan. 10 with the signing of a declaration under which India and Pakistan agreed to renounce force in the settlement of their disputes and to withdraw their troops to the position existing on Aug. 5, 1965, before the outbreak of hostilities between the two countries.

The main provisions of the Tashkent Declaration were as follows:

" (1) The Prime Minister of India and the President of Pakistan agree that both sides will exert all efforts to create good-neighbourly relations between India and Pakistan in accordance with the U.N. Charter.

"They reaffirm their obligation under the Charter not to have recourse to force and to settle their disputes through peaceful means. They considered that the interests of peace in their region and particularly in the Indo-Pakistan subcontinent and, indeed, the interests of the peoples of India and Pakistan, were not served by the continuance of tension between the two countries.

"It was against this background that Jammu and Kashmir was discussed, and each of the sides set forth its respective position."

(2) All armed personnel of the two countries would be withdrawn not later than Feb. 25, 1966, to the positions they held prior to Aug. 5, 1965, and both sides would observe the cease-fire terms on the cease-fire line.

(3) Relations between India and Pakistan would be based on the principle of non-interference in the internal affairs of each other.

(4) Both sides would discourage any propaganda directed against the other country.

(5) The normal functioning of diplomatic missions of both countries would be restored, and the High Commissioners of both countries would return to their posts.

(6) Measures towards the restoration of economic and trade relations, communications and cultural exchanges would be considered, and steps taken to implement the existing agreements between India and Pakistan.

(7) Prisoners of war would be repatriated.

(8) Discussions would continue relating to the problems of refugees and evictions of illegal immigrants. "Both sides will create conditions which will prevent the exodus of the people."

(9) "The Prime Minister of India and the President of Pakistan have agreed that the sides will continue meetings both at the highest and at other levels on matters of direct concern to both countries. Both sides have recognized the need to set up joint Indo-Pakistan bodies which will report to their Governments in order to decide what further steps should be taken."

Within a few hours of the signing of the Indo-Pakistan Declaration Mr. Shastri, who was 61, died suddenly in the early hours of Jan. 11, 1966.

Following unsuccessful talks at ministerial level [in accordance with the Tashkent Declaration] held in Rawalpindi on March 1-2, diplomatic exchanges between India and Pakistan on the possibility of holding further talks continued throughout the spring and summer. These led to no result, however, as Pakistan maintained that the most important issue to be discussed was that of Kashmir, whereas the Indian Government continued to uphold its view that Kashmir was an integral part of India.

Both India and Pakistan made repeated allegations that the other was violating the cease-fire agreement.

A threatening situation developed in the second half of August 1966, when India and Pakistan accused each other of concentrating troops on the border and along the cease-fire line in Kashmir. At the Indian Government's suggestion, talks took place in New Delhi on Sept. 13-14 between General P. P. Kumaramangalam (the Indian Chief of Army Staff) and Lieut.-General A. M. Yahya Khan (the Pakistani C.-in-C. designate) on means of lessening tension on the border. It was agreed that troop movements near the border should be avoided, and that troops should be confined as far as possible to peacetime stations; if it became necessary to move troops near the border, however, the country concerned would give advance notice to the other.

VIII. THE BREAKDOWN OF PRESIDENT AYUB KHAN'S REGIME, 1969

Latent dissatisfaction with President Ayub Khan's regime increased between 1966 and 1969, when demands for democratic rights in West Pakistan and for autonomy for East Pakistan led to a gradual breakdown of law and order, the proclamation of martial law and the replacement of President Ayub Khan by General Yahya Khan as Head of State.

STUDENT PROTESTS AND MR. BHUTTO'S AGITATION IN WEST PAKISTAN

A major political crisis developed in West Pakistan in October 1968 when students began agitating for educational reforms, demanding the repeal of the University Ordinance (which, *inter alia,* restricted student political activity and provided for the forfeiture of their degrees by graduates accused of subversive activities), the reduction of tuition fees and changes in the examination system. Their agitation, which began with sporadic strikes at Karachi University, was at first peaceful but became increasingly violent as it merged with a propaganda campaign against the regime by Mr. Zulfiqar Ali Bhutto, who was making a speaking tour of West Pakistan at the time. Mr. Bhutto had been Foreign Minister in 1963 but had disagreed with President Ayub Khan, and subsequently left the Government in 1966, denouncing President Ayub's rule as "a dictatorship under the label of democracy". Mr. Bhutto consequently formed his own party, the left-wing People's Party. When President Ayub Khan arrived for a visit to Peshawar on Nov. 9 police had to use strong measures to disperse students demonstrating against him, and at a public meeting on the following day a young student fired two shots close to the platform on which the President was sitting, but no one was hit.

Mr. Bhutto was arrested under the emergency regulations on Nov. 13 on a charge of inciting the students to violence, and riots occurred in many cities of West Pakistan following the arrest. Fourteen others were arrested at the same time, including seven members of the People's Party and five members of the left-wing National Awami Party. More clashes between police and students ensued, but by Nov. 14–15 the trouble had temporarily subsided, a number of student and Opposition leaders having been arrested and all colleges and schools having been temporarily closed.

The anti-Government agitation revived on Nov. 25, 1968, when protest demonstrations against the arrests of the Opposition leaders took place in Karachi, Lahore, Rawalpindi and Peshawar, organized by the Pakistan Democratic Movement, an alliance of five Opposition parties—the Awami League (which was moderate Socialist in outlook), the Council Moslem League (the faction of the Moslem League which had gone into opposition after the revival of political parties in 1962—see page 80), the *Nizam-i-Islam* (the liberal Islamic party), the ultra-orthodox *Jamaat-i-Islami,* and the East Pakistan National Democratic Front.

AGITATION FOR AUTONOMY IN EAST PAKISTAN

The agitation, which had hitherto been confined to West Pakistan, spread to East Pakistan on Dec. 7, 1968, with general strikes in East Pakistan called by the Opposition parties and clashes between police and demonstrators.

About the economic reasons for the upheaval, the *Financial Times* wrote on March 18, 1969: "East Pakistan is poorer and more overcrowded than almost any other major under-developed nation in the world. . . . When Pakistan split off from India in 1947 the East Wing of the new country had slightly more industry than the West. . . . The situation began to change when the Moslem businessmen of Bombay started the wholesale transfer of their businesses and capital to Karachi a year or two after partition. It got worse when Pakistan failed to follow India's devaluation of the rupee in line with sterling in 1949, thereby effectively cutting off East Pakistan from its natural market, the jute milling industry of West Bengal. . . . By 1959, according to the economists in the provincial planning department in Dacca, East Pakistanis were on average 20 per cent worse off than their less numerous compatriots in the West. By 1968 the disparity had widened (according to the same sources) to 40 per cent. . . . 1968 was, in point of fact, a peculiarly bad year for East Pakistan, with the destruction of over 1,000,000 tons of rice by floods and an absolute decline in the province's *per capita* income. . . ."

For some years prior to the crisis, demands had repeatedly been put forward in East Pakistan for full regional autonomy. Although East Pakistan contained 55 per cent of the country's population, and supplied a large part of Pakistan's foreign exchange by its jute exports, it had often been alleged that the region was under-represented in the armed forces, the judiciary and the Civil Service, and was receiving less than its fair share of development funds. Feeling on this issue had been greatly intensified by the war with India [see page 90], when for 17 days East Pakistan was cut off from contact with West Pakistan and was defended by only one Army division. The following six-point programme for regional autonomy was issued on Feb. 12, 1966, by Sheikh Mujibur Rahman, president of the Awami League, the strongest party in the region:

(1) Establishment of a federal form of government, with a Parliament directly elected by adult suffrage.

(2) The Federal Government would control only defence and foreign policy, leaving all other subjects to the federating States of East and West Pakistan.

(3) To stop the movement of capital from East to West Pakistan, either separate currencies or separate fiscal policies would be established.

(4) The Federal Government would share in State taxes for meeting its expenses, but would itself have no powers of taxation.

(5) Each of the federating States would be empowered to enter into trade agreements with foreign countries, and would have full control over its earned foreign exchange.

(6) The States would have their own militia or paramilitary forces.

President Ayub Khan denounced the autonomist movement as aimed at the disruption of Pakistan and the unification of East Pakistan and West Bengal as an independent State, and declared that the country would accept the challenge of a civil war if one were forced upon it. Sheikh Rahman was arrested on April 18, 1966, subsequently released, and rearrested on May 9 under the emergency regulations.

A general strike had subsequently been called by the Awami League on June 6, 1966, in Dacca and Narayanganj, where there were violent demonstrations in favour of regional autonomy. 28 people were arrested in January 1967 on charges of conspiring to bring about the secession of East Pakistan, including a naval officer, three senior civil servants and a number of non-commissioned officers, seamen and civilians.

The leaders of eight Opposition parties, meeting in Dacca on Jan. 8, 1969, formed the Democratic Action Committee, with the aim of replacing the "one-man dictatorship" which had "brought degradation and ruin to the country" and restoring democracy by means of a non-violent and disciplined mass movement. The demands of the committee, which included the five parties of the Pakistan Democractic Movement but not the National Awami Party, were: the abolition of the system of indirect election of the President, National Assembly and Provincial Assemblies through a college of "Basic Democrats", who, it was alleged, could easily be bribed or intimidated; the lifting of the emergency regulations introduced during the war with India in 1965 [see page 90], which permitted detention without trial; the removal of restrictions on the freedom of the Press; full autonomy for East Pakistan; and the establishment of a subfederation in West Pakistan.

GROWING DISORDER IN BOTH WINGS

The national executive of the Pakistan Trade Union Council sent a memorandum to President Ayub on Jan. 15, 1969, demanding the nationalization of all industries, banks and insurance companies and the appointment of a commission to report on the labour laws. The first of a series of "protest days" called by the Democratic Action

Committee was observed on Jan. 17 by demonstrations throughout the country, the only serious disturbances occurring in Dacca, where many students were injured in clashes with the police. On Jan. 20, the death of a student in a demonstration against "police excesses" set off a wave of protests which in the next 10 days virtually developed into a national uprising.

Faced with growing disorder throughout the country, President Ayub Khan offered on Feb. 1 to negotiate with the Opposition on constitutional changes; lifted the state of emergency on Feb. 17; ordered the release of Mr. Bhutto and other political prisoners; and announced on Feb. 21 that he would not seek re-election as President. Talks between the President and Opposition leaders opened in Rawalpindi on Feb. 26, at the conclusion of which President Ayub Khan announced on March 13 his acceptance of their two fundamental demands—parliamentary government with regional autonomy, and direct elections to the National and Provincial Assemblies.

During March 1969 an unprecedented wave of strikes occurred in both Wings of Pakistan. Those in East Pakistan were more violent and more widespread and resulted in a virtual breakdown of all authority. The students, who had almost total control of Dacca, demanded on March 3 the resignation of all the 40,000 Basic Democrats who formed both the electoral college and the members of local authorities in the province. Two Basic Democrats were murdered and others consequently hastened to resign. They were replaced by "People's Councils", the election of which was organized by students.

Rioting and mass strikes nevertheless continued in both West and East Pakistan, and in rural areas of the latter there was a virtual peasant revolt in which many supporters of the regime were murdered, since with the resignation of the Basic Democrats the whole system of local government collapsed, and in many villages the peasantry took advantage of the fact to attack unpopular persons. Victims of the mob attacks included Basic Democrats (often the local landlords and moneylenders), Moslem League members, unpopular police officials, rent collectors, and "foreign intruders" from West Pakistan, but in many cases the murders which occurred were believed to be the result of local feuds unconnected with politics.

As the provincial and local authorities were either unable or made little attempt to maintain order, the Awami League and the students took the initiative, the students forming "peace committees" which travelled through the country appealing for order and achieved some success in persuading "people's courts" to fine Basic Democrats and Moslem League members instead of killing them; a student leader said on March 19 that "they are paying up in their thousands rather than have their houses burned".

PRESIDENT AYUB KHAN'S RESIGNATION

Faced with this breakdown of law and order in many parts of the country, President Ayub Khan announced his resignation on March 25, 1969. Martial law was proclaimed, with the result that order was restored without difficulty. General Yahya Khan (the Commander-in-Chief of the Army), who had been appointed Chief Martial Law Administrator, assumed the Presidency on March 31 with the explanation that it was necessary to assume the office of Head of State until a new Constitution was framed. On April 3 he formed a Council of Administration consisting of the three Deputy Chief Martial Law Administrators, with himself as chairman.

The new President issued on April 4 the Provisional Constitution Order, which provided that notwithstanding its abrogation Pakistan should be governed as nearly as possible in accordance with the 1962 Constitution [see page 79]. The Order suspended the sections of the Constitution relating to fundamental rights, however; directed that no legal proceedings might be taken for the enforcement of those rights; and reaffirmed that the courts might not question any order issued or sentence passed by a military court under the martial law regulations.

In order to dispel fears that the reintroduction of the 1962 Constitution involved a return to the unpopular Basic Democracies system, Radio Pakistan announced on April 8 that President Yahya Khan had ordered an investigation of the system; that committees would be established at district and divisional levels to examine the causes of public resentment against the Basic Democrats and local government officials; and that any non-functioning Basic Democracies would not be revived.

On April 10 the President gave an assurance that elections to a

Constituent Assembly would be held on a basis of direct adult franchise.

Talks were held in April–July 1969 with party leaders on constitutional and political problems, and proposals were put forward for reforms of the Civil Service, the police, labour conditions and education. A number of civilian Ministers were appointed to the Administration, and Mr. Justice Abdus Sattar was made Chief Election Commissioner to prepare for general elections within 12–18 months.

In June 1969 four right-wing parties—the Justice Party (formed in March under Air Marshal Asghar Khan), the National Democratic Front (led by Mr. Nurul Amin), the *Nizam-i-Islam* (led by ex-Prime Minister Chaudhri Mohammad Ali) and the West Pakistan Awami League (under Nawabzada Nasrullah Khan)—merged to form the Pakistan Democratic Party, with Mr. Nurul Amin as president.

CONSTITUTIONAL DEVELOPMENTS

In a nation-wide broadcast on Nov. 28, 1969, President Yahya Khan announced far-reaching constitutional developments, outlining in his speech the legal framework for the restoration of a Federal parliamentary system; the holding of general elections on Oct. 5, 1970, on the basis of "one man, one vote"; the Constitution-making task of the newly elected National Assembly, which would have to be completed within 120 days, failing which the Assembly would be dissolved and a new National Assembly elected; the conferment of maximum autonomy on the provinces consistent with the maintenance of a strong Federation; the ending of the One-Unit system for West Pakistan and the restoration of its separate provinces; and permission for the resumption of unrestricted political activity as from Jan. 1, 1970.

In preparation for the resumption of political activities from the beginning of 1970, a Regulation was promulgated in December 1969 by President Yahya Khan, in his capacity as Chief Martial Law Administrator, laying down rules and guidance for the conduct of political campaigning. The Regulation laid down *inter alia* that "no political party shall propagate opinions or act in a manner prejudicial to the ideology, integrity or security of Pakistan"; that the interests of the common man would be protected against the acquisition of political power through the use of money, force or coercion; that freedom of the Press would be fully protected; and that any action which might amount to causing obstruction in the way of holding general elections would constitute an offence under the Regulation.

In conformity with the reforms announced in November 1969 [see above], full-scale political activity in Pakistan—including the lifting of all restrictions on public meetings and processions—was resumed on Jan. 1, 1970, in preparation for general elections originally scheduled to take place in October 1970 [see below] but which had to be postponed to December because of the disruption caused by exceptionally severe floods in East Pakistan, which by that date had claimed about 100 lives and made hundreds of thousands of people homeless.

In a broadcast on March 28, 1970, the President announced that the Legal Framework Order, 1970, to be published on March 29, would lay down the basic principles for the future Constitution of Pakistan [see below]; that the One-Unit system would be ended by July 1 in West Pakistan; that the National Assembly to be elected would consist of 313 members, of which 13 seats would be reserved for women; and that provincial elections would be held not later than Oct. 22, 1970. "The main objective that I have placed before myself," President Yahya Khan declared, "is the peaceful transfer of power to the people."

The Legal Framework Order, 1970, in laying down the fundamental principles which would be incorporated in the new Constitution, stated *inter alia*:

(1) The National Assembly would consist of 313 members, of whom 300 would be elected to fill general seats and 13 to fill seats reserved for women. East Pakistan would hold the largest number of seats.

(2) There would be a Provincial Assembly for each province, consisting of a number of members elected to fill general seats and a number to fill seats reserved for women. East Pakistan would again hold the largest number of seats.

(3) Polling for election to the National Assembly would commence on Oct. 5, 1970, and for the Provincial Assemblies not later than Oct. 22, 1970.

(4) The Constitution would be so framed as to embody the following fundamental principles:

101

"(i) Pakistan shall be a Federal Republic to be known as the Islamic Republic of Pakistan. . . .

"(ii) *(a)* Islamic theology, which is the basis for the creation of Pakistan, shall be preserved.

"(b) The Head of State shall be a Moslem.

"(iii) *(a)* Adherence to fundamental principles of democracy shall be ensured by providing direct and free periodical elections to the Federal and Provincial legislatures on the basis of population and adult franchise.

"(b) The fundamental rights of the citizens shall be laid down and guaranteed.

"(c) The independence of the judiciary . . . shall be secured.

" (iv) All powers, including legislative, administrative and financial, shall be so distributed between the Federal Government and the provinces that the provinces shall have maximum autonomy, that is to say maximum legislative, administrative and financial powers; but the Federal Government shall also have adequate powers, including legislative, administrative and financial powers, to discharge its responsibilities in relation to external and internal affairs and to preserve the independence and territorial integrity of the country.

"(v) It shall be ensured that

"(a) the people of all areas in Pakistan shall be enabled to participate fully in all forms of national activities; and

"(b) within a specified period, economic and all other disparities between the provinces and between different areas in a province are removed by the adoption of statutory and other measures."

(5) "The Constitution shall contain in its preamble an affirmation that:

"(i) The Moslems of Pakistan shall be enabled, individually and collectively, to order their lives in accordance with the teachings of Islam as set out in the Holy Koran and Sunna; and

"(ii) The minorities shall be free to profess and practise their religions freely, and to enjoy all rights, privileges and protection due to them as citizens of Pakistan."

(6) "The Constitution shall provide that

"(i) the National Assembly, constituted under this Order, shall:

"(*a*) be the first legislature of the Federation for the full term if the Legislature of the Federation consists of one House; and

"(*b*) be the first Lower House of the legislature of the Federation for the full term if the legislature of the Federation consists of two Houses.

"(ii) the Provincial Assemblies elected in accordance with this Order shall be the first legislatures of the respective provinces for the full term."

(7) "The National Assembly shall frame the Constitution in the

form of a Bill to be called the Constitution Bill within a period of 120 days from the date of its first meeting, and on its failure to do so shall stand dissolved."

In implementation of the policy announced by President Yahya Khan in his Addresses to the Nation in March and the previous November [see pages 100, 101] a Presidential Order was issued in April dissolving the One-Unit structure in West Pakistan and reviving the four former provinces of the Punjab, Sind, Baluchistan and the North-West Frontier Province. Under the Order, Bahawalpur went to the Punjab, Karachi to Sind, and Las Bela to Baluchistan.

IX. PAKISTAN'S EAST WING BECOMES INDEPENDENT BANGLADESH

THE GENERAL ELECTIONS OF 1970

The first general elections ever held in Pakistan on a basis of "one man, one vote" took place on Dec. 7, 1970, and resulted in an overwhelming victory for the Awami League, led by Sheikh Mujibur Rahman, in East Pakistan, and a large majority for the Pakistan People's Party, led by Mr. Zulfiqar Ali Bhutto, in West Pakistan. Out of a total of 291 seats, the Awami League gained 151 and the Pakistan People's Party 81.

In all, 23 parties put forward 1,237 candidates for the 291 seats, and there were also 391 Independent candidates. Over 60 candidates in East Pakistan withdrew on the eve of the elections, ostensibly as a protest against the Government's handling of relief operations in the Ganges delta (after the cyclone disaster of November 1970—see page 116); they were generally believed to have done so, however, in order to avoid a humiliating defeat by the Awami League.

In a broadcast before the elections, President Yahya Khan had reminded the electorate on Dec. 3, 1970, that martial law remained in force and that the Army would ensure that order was maintained. Apart from a few incidents, however, the election campaign and the voting took place in a peaceful atmosphere, and all parties, including those which were defeated, agreed that the elections were both free and fair. There was a heavy poll which surpassed 90 per cent in some areas, and women, who were voting for the first time, turned out in large numbers.

RESULTS OF 1970 GENERAL ELECTIONS

	East Pakistan	Punjab	Sind	NWFP	Baluch-istan	Total
Awami League	151 (153)	— (2)	— (2)	— (2)	— (1)	151 (160)
Pakistan People's Party	— (—)	62 (77)	18 (25)	1 (16)	— (1)	81 (119)
Council Moslem League	— (50)	7 (50)	— (12)	— (5)	— (2)	7 (119)
Ahle Sunnat	— (—)	4 (39)	3 (8)	— (—)	— (1)	7 (48)
Jamaat-i-Islami	— (69)	1 (43)	2 (19)	1 (15)	— (2)	4 (148)
Qayyum Moslem League	— (65)	1 (34)	1 (12)	7 (17)	— (4)	9 (132)
Convention Moslem League	— (93)	2 (24)	— (6)	— (1)	— (—)	2 (124)
Pakistan Democratic Party	1 (81)	— (21)	— (3)	— (2)	— (1)	1 (108)
National Awami Party (Wali Group)	— (39)	— (—)	— (6)	3 (16)	3 (3)	6 (64)
Jamiat-i-Ulema-i-Pakistan (Hazarvi Group)	— (13)	— (47)	— (20)	6 (19)	1 (4)	7 (103)
Independents	1 (109)	5 (114)	3 (46)	7 (45)	— (5)	16 (319)
Total	153	82	27	25	4	291

Note. The figures in parentheses indicate the number of candidates put up by the party.

In nine constituencies in East Pakistan voting had to be postponed until Jan. 17, 1971, due to the effects of the cyclone disaster.

One of the main issues in the elections was the demand for the release of political prisoners, which was pressed in particular by Mr. Bhutto; the editor of the Pakistan People's Party's weekly was arrested in consequence in October on a charge of "publishing material designed to malign and defame the Chief Martial Law Administrator". President Yahya Khan granted an amnesty on Dec. 17 to all persons imprisoned for "offences relating to agitational activity", over 1,000 prisoners subsequently being released. Two journalists, however, one of them an Awami League official, were arrested on Dec. 21 under the martial law regulations for writing articles criticizing President Yahya Khan.

As the Awami League had an absolute majority of the 291 seats in the National Assembly for which elections had been held, and was expected to win the nine others for which voting had been postponed and the seven women's seats for East Pakistan, its leaders maintained that the Constitution must be based on its six-point formula. This attitude led to a heated controversy between Sheikh Mujibur and Mr. Bhutto, who contended that the Constitution must receive the assent of all the provinces.

Addressing a vast crowd estimated at 2,000,000 people in Dacca on Jan. 3, 1971, Sheikh Mujibur declared that the people of East Pakistan had given a clear verdict on the six points, and the future Constitution of the country would be framed on the basis of those points alone. The people were ready to accept the Constitution, which would be prepared by their elected representatives, and would launch a strong mass movement if anyone opposed the framing of the Constitution. He added, however, that his party would not frame the Constitution alone, even though it was in a majority in the Assembly.

Sheikh Mujibur, who contested two Dacca constituencies, was returned in both with majorities of 120,000 and 94,000, while most of the other Awami League candidates received similar great majorities. The party fought the elections on the basis of the six-point programme for autonomy for East Pakistan put forward by Sheikh Mujibur in 1966 [see page 96].

The Pakistan People's Party, founded by Mr. Bhutto in 1967 [see page 95], won a large majority of the seats in the Punjab and Sind;

it did not contest any seats in East Pakistan, and had little success in the other two provinces. Mr. Bhutto was returned in five of the six constituencies which he contested, and his party won all eight Rawalpindi seats and all the four Lahore seats. Its victory in the Punjab and Sind was attributed to the party's combination of economic radicalism and anti-Indian nationalism and to the appeal of Mr. Bhutto's dynamic personality, especially to younger voters.

The results of the elections to the Provincial Assemblies held on Dec. 17 were similar to those in the elections to the National Assembly. The Awami League obtained an overwhelming majority in East Pakistan; the Pakistan People's Party had a large majority in the Punjab and a smaller majority in Sind; and the National Awami Party was the largest group in the North-West Frontier Province and Baluchistan Assemblies, though it did not obtain a majority in either.

THE BUILD-UP TO CIVIL WAR IN EAST PAKISTAN, DECEMBER 1970–MARCH 1971

The general elections in Pakistan were followed by an extremely tense political situation. The Awami League had won practically every seat in East Pakistan, and with its total of 151 seats had an overall majority in the National Assembly; Mr. Bhutto's Pakistan People's Party (PPP), with 81 seats, emerged as by far the largest and most important party in West Pakistan, but without a majority in the Assembly. [Of the two Wings of the country, which were separated by 1,000 miles of Indian territory, East Pakistan had more than half the country's total population.]

With the National Assembly due to meet in Dacca for its first session on March 3, 1971, President Yahya Khan had separate meetings at the end of January with Sheikh Mujibur Rahman and Mr. Bhutto in an attempt to resolve the differences between the Awami League and the PPP on the country's future Constitution, whilst the two political leaders also met on several occasions at the beginning of February. Throughout these discussions, however, Sheikh Mujibur adhered unequivocally to the Six Points on which the Awami League had fought the general election [see page 96]—involving, if implemented, almost complete independence of the Centre for East Pakistan, as for the other provincial units, except in the fields of defence and foreign affairs.

On Feb. 17 Mr. Bhutto declared that "under present circumstances" it was pointless for the PPP to attend the inaugural session of the National Assembly, as the party did not wish to make the journey to Dacca merely to endorse a Constitution which they would have no say in framing [since the Awami League had an overall majority in the Assembly]. If a "viable" Constitution was to be framed for Pakistan, he emphasized, the PPP must have a hand in its framing. The Awami League, however, he asserted, had shown itself completely inflexible, and had insisted that there could be no room for compromise and that a Constitution must be based on its Six-Point programme. Mr. Bhutto added that the PPP had tried its best to work out some agreed settlement and understanding with the Awami League but that the latter's attitude left no room for further negotiation.

Sheikh Mujibur on Feb. 24 described as "utterly false" the allegation that the Awami League was seeking to impose its Six-Point programme on West Pakistan.

The Pakistan Moslem League also announced that it would not attend the opening session of the Assembly.

President Yahya Khan on Feb. 21 announced the dissolution of Pakistan's all-civilian Cabinet, "in view of the situation prevailing in the country", and then, on March 1, broadcast his decision to postpone indefinitely the opening of the National Assembly, in order to allow the leaders time to settle the question of framing a Constitution. The President said in his broadcast:

"Needless to say, I took this decision to postpone the date of the National Assembly with a heavy heart. One has, however, to look at the practical aspects of such problems. I realized that, with so many representatives of the people of West Pakistan keeping away from the Assembly, if we were to go ahead with the inaugural session on March 3 the Assembly itself could have disintegrated and the entire effort made for the smooth transfer of power would have been wasted.

"I wish to make a solemn promise to the people of Pakistan that, as soon as circumstances become conducive to Constitution-making, I will have no hesitation in calling a session of the Assembly immediately. . . ."

On the same day the appointment of Martial Law Administrators for the various provinces was announced, all these concurrently assuming the functions of Provincial Governors in their respective provinces.

The decision to postpone the Assembly session led to a general strike in Dacca and angry demonstrations, resulting in several casualties.

President Yahya Khan subsequently announced on March 6 that the inaugural session of the Assembly would take place on March 25. However, Sheikh Mujibur put forward the following conditions for the Awami League's participation in the Assembly session: (1) the withdrawal of martial law; (2) the return of troops to barracks; (3) an inquiry into killings which, he alleged, had taken place in East Pakistan; (4) transfer of power to the elected representatives of the people. While calling for a continued *hartal* (general strike) in Government offices and the law courts until these conditions were accepted, and urging the people of East Pakistan to stop payment of taxes and revenues to the Government until power was transferred to the people's representatives, Sheikh Mujibur said there was "still time for us to live as brothers if things are settled peacefully".

In an attempt to save the country from a total split, President Yahya Khan arrived in Dacca on March 15 for talks with Sheikh Mujibur Rahman, the strictest security precautions being taken by the Army. East Pakistan was by then in its third week of strikes and civil disobedience to force the Central Government to meet the Awami League's demands; all civil servants, including judges, were on strike, as well as workers in key defence establishments, despite a martial law regulation ordering them to return to work on penalty of 10 years' imprisonment if they failed to do so. Under a series of directives issued by Sheikh Mujibur Rahman, no taxes or revenues were to be paid to the Central Government; radio, television and newspapers were instructed to ignore the martial law censorship regulations; telephone communications with places outside East Pakistan were cut, only press telegrams being allowed to be sent; teleprinter circuits with West Pakistan remained open for only one hour a day for the service messages of banks; and the police, port authorities and postal and telegraph authorities were instructed to continue functioning for the benefit of the people of East Pakistan but to do nothing that could help the Central Government. At the same time Sheikh Mujibur called on the people of East Pakistan to be ready for "sacrifice" and to resist force "by all possible means".

President Yahya and Sheikh Mujibur had talks in strict secrecy on March 16 and again on the following day, but on March 18 it appeared that the negotiations had broken down when Sheikh Mujibur rejected the President's offer to set up a commission "to inquire into the circumstances which led to the calling out of the Army in aid of civil powers in East Pakistan". [As stated above, an inquiry into alleged killings by the armed forces had been one of the four demands put forward by the Awami League on March 7.] In rejecting the President's offer, Sheikh Mujibur said that he objected to the terms of reference of the proposed commission and declared: "Such a commission can serve no useful purpose. Indeed, such an inquiry would not be a genuine inquiry aimed at arriving at the truth but would be a mere device to mislead people. The people of Bengal will not cooperate with such a commission in any respect. . . ."

Mr. Bhutto arrived in Dacca on March 21 to participate in the talks between the President and Sheikh Mujibur, but on the following day it became apparent that they had broken down in complete failure when President Yahya Khan, after an hour-long meeting between Sheikh Mujibur and Mr. Bhutto, announced that he had again postponed the inaugural session of the National Assembly to an unspecified date "in consultation with the leaders of both Wings of Pakistan and with a view to facilitating and enlarging the area of agreement among the political parties". Sheikh Mujibur told journalists after the meeting that he had "made it clear that I shall not sit in the Assembly unless our four demands are fulfilled".

With East Pakistan on the brink of secession, President Yahya Khan and Mr. Bhutto flew back to West Pakistan on March 25. On the same day Sheikh Mujibur, addressing large crowds in Dacca, told them to prepare themselves for the "supreme sacrifice", after which he issued a series of directives to commercial firms, the effect of which was to emphasize that the separation of East Pakistan from the west Wing was imminent, if not actually in operation.

With the law and order situation in East Pakistan deteriorating, there had been a build-up of troops in the province for some time previously. While no details of troop movements were given in Pakistan itself, the Press Trust of India (PTI) reported on March 25 that West Pakistan troops were being landed by sea at Chittagong and were also arriving by air in Dacca.

THE OUTBREAK OF CIVIL WAR

Full-scale civil war erupted in East Pakistan on March 26, 1971, when a clandestine radio broadcast announced the proclamation by Sheikh Mujibur Rahman and the Awami League of the "sovereign independent people's republic of Bangladesh". The broadcast, which was monitored in India, said that heavy fighting was in progress at Chittagong, Comilla, Sylhet, Jessore, Barisal and Khulna, where West Pakistan forces were claimed to be surrounded by troops of the East Bengal Regiment, the East Pakistan Rifles and the "entire" police force. Calls were made to the people of Bangladesh ("Bengal Nation") to continue the struggle for independence "until the last enemy soldier had vanished", and Sheikh Mujibur—who was said to have gone underground—was described as "the only leader of independent Bangladesh", whose orders should be obeyed to save the country from "the ruthless dictatorship of the West Pakistanis". Another clandestine broadcast said that Bangladesh had appealed to the United Nations and to the Afro-Asian countries for help in its "struggle for freedom".

On the same day President Yahya Khan outlawed the Awami League, placed a ban on political activity throughout Pakistan, and imposed complete press censorship.

With official communications between East Pakistan and the rest of the world cut, and a rigorous press censorship in force, the only news of the civil war in the province came from clandestine radio broadcasts, from refugees crossing into India, from statements by foreign press correspondents after they had left East Pakistan for the outside world, and from Indian newspapers. Completely contradictory reports about the fighting, moreover, were given on the one hand by official Pakistani statements and broadcasts and on the other by clandestine broadcasts monitored in India and by the Indian Press. Reports reaching Calcutta on March 28-29, however, spoke of fierce fighting in Dacca, Rangpur, Comilla and other centres in East Paki-

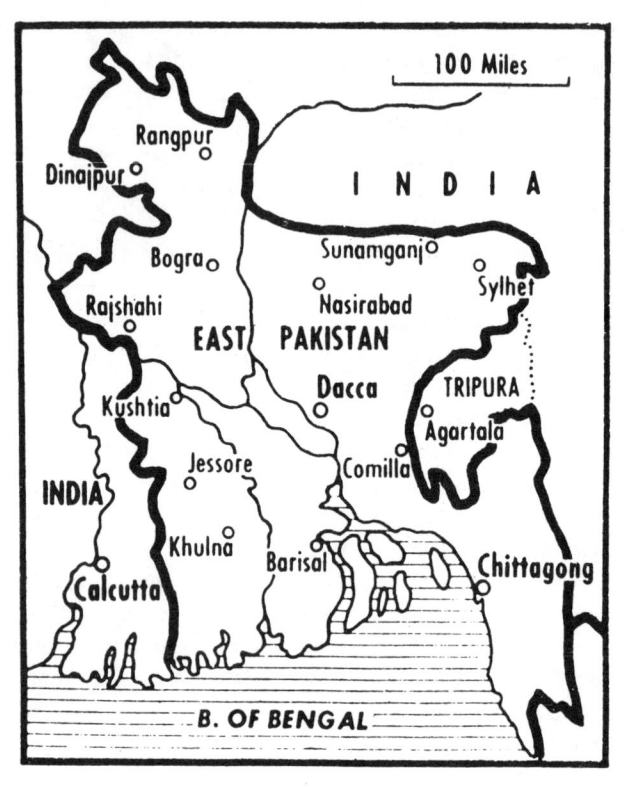

(Reproduced by permission from *The Times*.)

stan; the clandestine Bangladesh radio said on March 27 that the Pakistan Air Force had bombed Dacca, Comilla and Khulna and alleged that Dacca University—an Awami League stronghold—had been destroyed by shelling by Pakistan Army tanks, with heavy casualties among students.

Two journalists, Mr. Simon Dring of *The Daily Telegraph* and Mr. Michel Laurent, an Associated Press photographer, both of whom had evaded the round-up and deportation of press correspondents in the province, made an extensive tour of Dacca, describing it later as "a crushed and frightened city" after "24 hours of shelling by the

Pakistan Army", and saying that as many as 7,000 were dead and that large areas had been levelled.

Despite official Pakistani statements to the contrary, it appeared that, at least during the first ten days of April, the Bangladesh forces were continuing to put up a stubborn resistance in a number of centres; all the main towns of East Pakistan, however, were in the hands of the Army within a relatively short time, and the secessionist forces, lightly armed in comparison with the regular troops, were being driven more and more into the remoter rural areas.

By April 12–13, press correspondents' reports from the Indo-Pakistan frontier area indicated that the Pakistan Army was everywhere on the offensive and fanning out in all directions north and west of Dacca, and that the resistance of the Bangladesh "liberation forces" was everywhere crumbling despite bitter last-ditch opposition in some areas.

Those towns—among them Jessore, Sylhet and Khulna—which for a time had been partially or wholly under secessionist control were firmly in the hands of the Regular Army, which also controlled all main roads and waterways, and to all intents and purposes the civil war ended on April 18 with the capture by the Pakistan Army of the village of Chuadanga, 300 yards from the Indian border, which had been proclaimed the provisional capital of Bangladesh.

With the Pakistan Army in complete control of the western frontier area bordering on India, all effective resistance by the Bangladesh "liberation army" had virtually ceased by April 18–19.

A clandestine radio broadcast on April 11 had announced the formation "somewhere in Bangladesh" of a six-member Cabinet of the "independent sovereign republic of Bangladesh", with Sheikh Mujibur Rahman as President.

The Bangladesh "Government" had set up its headquarters in the village of Chuadanga, only a few hundred yards from the Indian frontier, where on April 17, 1972, the "Democratic Republic of Bangladesh" was formally proclaimed. On the following day, however, when Chuadanga was occupied by the Pakistan Army, no trace was found of any of the members of the Cabinet.

The Government of India announced on April 2, 1971, that more than a quarter of a million refugees from East Pakistan had crossed into India since the civil war broke out.

DETERIORATION OF RELATIONS BETWEEN INDIA AND PAKISTAN FOLLOWING CIVIL WAR

Relations between India and Pakistan, already tense, deteriorated sharply in 1971 as a result of the civil war in East Pakistan, leading to acrimonious exchanges of Notes between the two countries and to numerous charges and countercharges by each side.

Mr. Swaran Singh, the Indian Minister of External Affairs, accused the Pakistan Army of "suppressing the people of East Pakistan" and said that "the Government of India cannot but be gravely concerned at events taking place so close to our borders", and on March 31, 1971, both Houses of the Indian Parliament passed a resolution, moved by the Prime Minister, Mrs. Gandhi, expressing "wholehearted sympathy and support" for the people of Bengal.

The acute friction between India and Pakistan was heightened by alleged incidents on the border of India and East Pakistan, and by the defection of the Pakistan Deputy High Commissioner in Calcutta, which was followed by the closing of the Pakistan Deputy High Commission in that city and of the Indian Deputy High Commission in Dacca (the staffs being later repatriated in August). At the same time vast numbers of refugees passed into India from East Pakistan on a scale unprecedented in any part of the world since World War II. By mid-June 1971 some 5,500,000–6,000,000 people had crossed the border.

The almost intolerable strain imposed both on the Central and the West Bengal Governments in receiving and providing minimal care for the vast numbers of refugees was aggravated by outbreaks of cholera among the refugees which claimed several thousand lives, but which were eventually halted by massive medical aid from the international community and U.N. organizations, as well as the efforts of the Indian authorities themselves.

In a Note to the Pakistan High Commission in Delhi on May 14, the Indian Government reserved the right to claim from the Pakistan Government "full satisfaction" in respect of the additional financial and other burdens incurred as a result of the mass influx of refugees from East Pakistan. The Note asserted that the refugees were "victims of a deliberate campaign of terror launched against them" by the Pakistani armed forces and accused the Pakistan Government of displaying "total indifference and unconcern" at the fate of the refugees.

President Yahya Khan issued a statement on May 21 urging *bona fide* Pakistani citizens who had "left their homes owing to disturbed conditions and for other reasons" to return to East Pakistan, and on June 10 offered a general amnesty.

Mrs. Gandhi said on June 17 that the refugees were "certainly not going to stay there in India permanently", and that the Government were "determined to send them back". Planes on June 15 began flying refugees from the border areas to 50 large camps in Madhya Pradesh, Orissa, Uttar Pradesh and Bihar, with the help of Soviet, British, Australian and U.S. aircraft.

Meanwhile, acute tension continued to exist on the border between India and East Pakistan, many charges being made by both sides during the months from April to July alleging border violations and acts of aggression by the other.

The Indian Defence Minister, Mr. Jagjivan Ram, told Indian Army units at Jullunder (Punjab) on June 20 that they should be prepared "to meet any eventuality that might arise because of the desperate acts" of Pakistan's military rulers. Alleging that Pakistan had been violating India's eastern borders, Mr. Ram declared: "We are a peace-loving country and we want to avoid war, but Pakistan is creating a situation where war may be thrust on us."

From time to time the Indian and foreign Press brought reports of activities inside East Pakistan by Bangladesh secessionist guerrillas, the *Mukti Bahini* (Liberation Army), previously known as the *Mukti Fouj*. The nucleus of the guerrilla forces consisted of soldiers of the East Bengal Regiment and the East Pakistan Rifles, which had reportedly rallied to the separatist cause in March virtually in a body, and all sector commanders and most of their subordinates were reported to be former officers of the Pakistan Army. Volunteers were also enrolled, especially for sabotage operations, from students and high school pupils, whilst guerrilla groups organized by the left-wing National Awami Party and the Communist Party of Bangladesh operated in the interior of East Pakistan independently of the *Mukti Bahini*.

Guerrilla activities were greatly intensified from August 1971 onwards. Then refugees entering India began to report that, as a reprisal for the guerrillas' activities, the Army and the *Razakars* (civilian militia) had let loose a reign of terror; Western correspondents in East Pakistan confirmed these reports, e.g. on Sept. 21 a *New York Times* correspondent wrote:

"The dozens of refugees interviewed by this correspondent today, all of whom fled into India from East Pakistan in the past week, describe the killing of civilians, rape and other acts of repression by the soldiers. . . . Nearly all the latest arrivals are Hindus, who said that the military regime was still making the Hindu minority its particular target. They said that the guerrillas were active in their areas, and that the Army carried out massive reprisals against civilians after every guerrilla raid. . . . According to the refugees, the Army leaves much of the 'dirty work' to its civilian collaborators—the *Razakars,* or Home Guards—it has armed, and to the supporters of right-wing religious political parties such as the Moslem League and *Jamaat-i-Islami.*"

The civil war had occurred before East Pakistan had recovered from the great cyclone disaster of November 1970—the worst of its kind in the twentieth century, the number of dead being estimated at 200,000—and in August 1971 heavy monsoon rains caused severe floods. Many West Bengal refugee camps were flooded, the breakdown in communications prevented food and supplies from reaching stricken areas, and a major famine was feared. Moreover, the refugee influx was causing serious social tensions in the border areas of West Bengal. A *Times* correspondent reported on Nov. 18: "A registered refugee who gets food rations from Government stocks is better fed than most landless labourers in the neighbourhood. Others living outside camps are being employed by landowners as farm labourers on wages much lower than those that must be paid to labourers from the locality. . . . This is causing resentment among the local working force."

In addition, the cost of maintaining the refugees was imposing an extremely heavy burden on India's economy. In October and November 1971 Mrs. Gandhi undertook a tour of six Western capitals—Brussels, Vienna, London, Washington, Paris and Bonn—during which she had talks with the leaders of the respective countries. In London she again emphasized her determination that "the vast majority of refugees must go back".

Mrs. Gandhi had on Sept. 27–29, 1971, also visited Moscow for talks. Soviet criticism of Pakistani policy in East Pakistan greatly increased after her visit.

Both India and Pakistan made repeated allegations in September and October that their territory had been shelled from the other side of the East Pakistan border, and during October the Indian Press claimed that the Pakistan Army was concentrated near the West Pakistan frontier; that new defence lines were being constructed on the border; and that the civilian population had been evacuated from a 500-mile stretch of the frontier opposite the Indian State of Rajasthan. President Yahya Khan, on the other hand, stated on Oct. 12 that a large number of Indian Air Force units and Army formations had been brought forward towards the West Pakistan border, and it was confirmed on Oct. 24 that the Army had taken over defence duties in the Rann of Kutch from the Border Security Force. Violations of the cease-fire line in Kashmir were also alleged.

U Thant (the United Nations Secretary-General) offered the use of his good offices in the "potentially dangerous situation" between India and Pakistan in a letter of Oct. 20 to President Yahya Khan and Mrs. Gandhi. President Yahya Khan replied the next day, welcoming U Thants' offer; however, Mrs. Gandhi, while also welcoming the offer, emphasized the Indian view that only a political settlement in East Pakistan could solve the problem and said: ". . . The root of the problem is the fate of 75,000,000 people of East Bengal and their inalienable rights. This is what must be kept in mind, instead of the present attempt to save the military regime. To side-track this main problem and to convert it into an Indo-Pakistani dispute can only aggravate tensions. . . . The problem of East Bengal can be solved only by peaceful negotiations between the military rulers of West Pakistan and the elected and accepted leaders of East Bengal. The first step towards opening of such negotiations is the release of Sheikh Mujibur Rahman. . . ."

While attacks on Pakistani forces were reported from almost all sectors of East Pakistan between Nov. 21 and Dec. 2, 1971, and were attributed by Pakistani official sources to Indian troops and by the Indians to the *Mukti Bahini,* fighting on the East Pakistan border was greatly intensified after Nov. 21, when the *Mukti Bahini* launched an offensive against Jessore, reportedly with Indian support (although Indian sources denied this). After further fighting on Nov. 29 in the Jessore region, Indian troops overran a hamlet west of Jessore, and it was reported that the head of the *Mukti Bahini* had set up headquarters near the town and that leaders of the Bangladesh movement had moved into the area in readiness to set up a Government in Jessore when it fell.

Finally, Indian troops were officially stated to have entered East Pakistan on Nov. 27, after Pakistani artillery had heavily shelled the Indian frontier towns of Hilli and Balurghat, the Indian Defence Minister giving the explanation that it was more effective to silence the guns from Pakistani territory.

President Yahya Khan proclaimed a state of emergency on Nov. 23, declaring that "a most critical situation has been created because Pakistan is faced with external aggression"; the practical implications of this proclamation were not clear, however, as the country had been under martial law since 1969. Mrs. Gandhi described the President's declaration as "the climax of his efforts to divert the attention of the world from Bangladesh and to put the blame on us for the situation which he himself has created", and said: "We shall refrain from taking a similar step, unless further aggression by Pakistan compels us to do so."

THE INDO-PAKISTAN WAR

The clashes between the Indian and Pakistani forces finally developed into open war on Dec. 3, 1971, when the Pakistan Air Force made a surprise attack on military airfields in western India. The main aims of the attack, it was believed, were to reduce the pressure on the forces in East Pakistan by creating a diversion in the west; to occupy territory in Kashmir and Rajasthan which could be used as a bargaining counter in negotiating a settlement in East Pakistan; and to secure the intervention of the great Powers or the U.N. Security Council.

Two hours before the Pakistani air raids in the west, Pakistani aircraft attacked the airfield at Agartala (Tripura) on Dec. 3 for the second consecutive day. Indian troops which had crossed the border on Dec. 2 forced the Pakistanis to withdraw artillery which had been shelling the town for the past three days, and took up positions just inside Pakistani territory.

On Dec. 4 India launched an integrated ground, air and naval offensive against East Pakistan. The Army, linking up with the *Mukti Bahini,* entered East Pakistan from five main directions, the aim being to divide the Pakistani units stationed round the border and to prevent them from uniting in defence of Dacca, which occupies a strong strategic position protected by the complex river system at the mouth of the Ganges and the Brahmaputra.

India announced on Dec. 6 that she had recognized the Provisional Government of Bangladesh, whereupon the Pakistan Government broke off diplomatic relations with India.

On Dec. 7 the advancing Indian troops achieved two major successes, capturing Sylhet and then Jessore.

Western journalists who visited Jessore described the tumultuous welcome which the Indian forces received from the Bengali population, and gave details of the ordeal to which the civilian population in the town had been subjected since April. An Italian missionary told reporters that during the week April 4–10 the streets and houses had been full of bodies of residents executed in batches by the soldiers and *Razakars,* and estimated that 10,000 people had been executed in and around Jessore, which normally has a population of about 60,000. Over half the population, including almost all the women, had fled to the countryside or to India during the occupation by the Pakistan Army; the Hindu community had disappeared, and many of the houses in the empty Hindu quarter had been demolished.

General Sam Manekshaw, the Indian Army Chief of Staff, broadcast on Dec. 7 an appeal to the Pakistan Army in East Pakistan to surrender "before it is too late", promising them good treatment. Pointing out that their Air Force was destroyed and the ports blocked, he warned them that "the *Mukti Bahini* and the people fighting for liberation have encircled you, and are all prepared to take revenge for the atrocities and cruelties you have committed".

The Indian Army continued to advance on all fronts in East Pakistan during the period Dec. 8–14, converging on Dacca towards the end of this period. The Army began shelling the city on Dec. 14, while aircraft attacked with rockets, meeting with virtually no resistance.

After long discussions with his Ministers the Governor of East Pakistan, Dr. A. M. Malik, wrote a letter tendering his resignation to President Yahya Khan in the afternoon of Dec. 14 in an air-raid shelter in his garden; his official residence had been destroyed in an air raid shortly before. He then took refuge with his family and his Ministers in the Intercontinental Hotel, which had been declared a neutral zone for foreigners, wounded soldiers and other non-combatants and was administered by the Red Cross. 16 senior officials, including the Inspector-General of Police, had already sought refuge in the hotel.

On Dec. 15 the Indian forces closed in on Dacca from all sides, and in the afternoon of that day General Amin Abdullah Khan Niazi, the Pakistani military commander, sent a message to General Manekshaw through the U.S. Consulate in Dacca and the U.S. Embassy in New Delhi proposing a cease-fire; in it he asked for facilities for regrouping his forces with their weapons in designated areas pending their repatriation to West Pakistan, a guarantee of safety for the paramilitary forces and for all those who had settled in East Pakistan since 1947, and an assurance that there would be no reprisals against those who had collaborated with the martial law authorities. In his reply, however, General Manekshaw insisted on the unconditional surrender of the Pakistani forces.

On the morning of Dec. 16 General Niazi was unable to inform General Manekshaw of his acceptance of these terms because communications at his headquarters had been put out of action by Indian bombing. A message was therefore sent to New Delhi through U.N. radio facilities, 10 minutes before General Manekshaw's ultimatum was due to expire, asking for a six-hour extension of the bombing pause and for an Indian staff officer to negotiate terms of surrender.

Major-General J. F. R. Jacob, Chief of Staff of the Eastern Command of the Indian Army, arrived by air, and discussions began at once. The surrender terms agreed upon between General Niazi and General Jacob provided that all Pakistani regular, paramilitary and civilian armed forces would lay down their arms, and guaranteed that they would be treated in accordance with the Geneva Conventions and that foreign nationals, ethnic minorities and personnel of West Pakistani origin would be protected.

An Indian battalion had already entered Dacca unopposed during the morning, and was joined in the afternoon by four more, including two battalions of the *Mukti Bahini;* they were greeted in the streets by thousands of jubilant Bengalis, who hugged and kissed the soldiers and garlanded them with flowers.

The signed surrender documents were presented to General Jagjit Singh Aurora (C.-in-C., Indian Eastern Command) on Dacca racecourse, while Indian troops held back cheering crowds.

Fighting continued at Khulna and in the Sylhet area until the morning of Dec. 17, as the Pakistani forces in these sectors had not by then received instructions. By Dec. 23, however, 89,000 regular and paramilitary troops had surrendered; they were not disarmed until they were taken to camps where full protection could be provided, as it was feared that the local population would take revenge on them. General Niazi and General Farman Ali Khan—Dr. Malik's military adviser, whose proposal for a cease-fire on Dec. 10 had been first agreed to and then countermanded by President Yahya Khan—were flown to India on Dec. 20, and a first group of 630 prisoners of war left Dacca for internment camps in India on Dec. 28. General Manekshaw had stated on the previous day that present plans were for all Pakistani prisoners of war to be moved to India by Jan. 15, 1972, and that he hoped that 25,000 Indian soldiers would have left Bangladesh by that date.

Fighting also continued on the West Pakistan border and on the cease-fire line in Kashmir until Dec. 17.

In a broadcast on Dec. 16 President Yahya Khan admitted defeat in East Pakistan, though without mentioning that the Army had surrendered, and declared that the war would go on: "We will continue to fight the enemy on every front, and also continue our efforts to form a representative Government in the country, which the enemy, by launching an attack, tried to set aside. According to the programme, the Constitution will be announced on Dec. 20. This guarantees the maximum autonomy to East Pakistan on the basis of one Pakistan, for whose establishment and protection the people of both Wings of the country sacrificed so much. A Central Government will be formed after this, and subsequently Provincial Governments will come into being. . . ."

Mrs. Gandhi shortly afterwards announced that she had ordered a unilateral cease-fire on the western front from 8 p.m. on Dec. 17, declaring that "India has no territorial ambitions" and that, Pakistani forces having surrendered and Bangladesh being free, "it is pointless

(*Economist*)

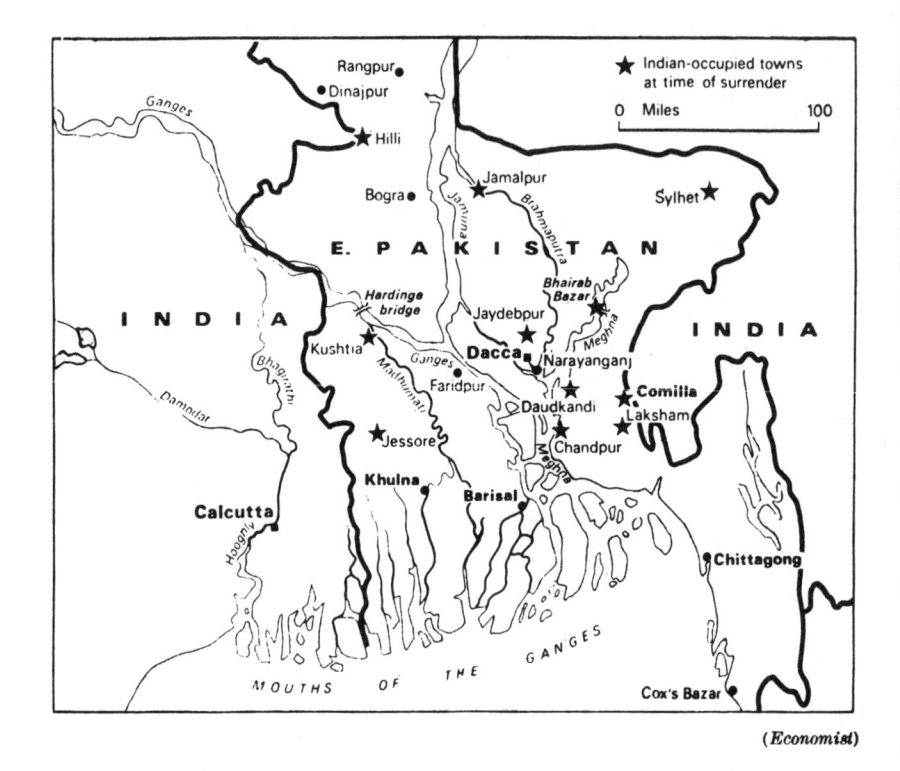

in our view to continue the present conflict". After this decision had been communicated to President Yahya Khan through the Swiss Embassy, he subsequently announced that he had also ordered a cease-fire to come into force at the same time.

Following the President's decision, the U.N. Security Council suspended its discussions about the war (previous attempts by the U.N. to bring about a cease-fire had resulted in failure), and after consultations met again on Dec. 22, when a compromise resolution was put forward by Argentina, Burundi, Japan, Nicaragua, Sierra Leone and Somalia.

The resolution called for strict observance of the cease-fire in all areas of conflict, and the withdrawal of all armed forces as soon as practicable to their respective territories and to positions which fully respected the cease-fire line in Kashmir. It also called on all countries to refrain from actions which might complicate the situation in the sub-continent; called on all those concerned to observe the Geneva Conventions of 1949 on the protection of wounded and sick prisoners of war and the civilian population; called for international assistance in the relief of refugees and their return in safety to their homes; and authorized the Secretary-General to appoint, if necessary, a special representative to lend his good offices for the solution of humanitarian problems.

The resolution was adopted by 13 votes to none, with Poland and the Soviet Union abstaining. The Chinese delegation, while voting for the resolution, expressed dissatisfaction with it.

Meanwhile, however, violent demonstrations against the military regime in West Pakistan, beginning on Dec. 18, had led to the resignation of President Yahya Khan, in succession to whom Mr. Bhutto was sworn in as Pakistan's new President on Dec. 20.

BANGLADESH GOVERNMENT ESTABLISHED IN DACCA

The city of Dacca was in a state of virtual anarchy after the surrender of the Pakistan Army, elements of the *Mukti Bahini* using the opportunity to take revenge on "collaborators" and especially on the *Razakars*. Violence was provoked largely by massacres reported to have been carried out by the soldiers and the *Razakars* from March 1971 to the time of surrender. The mutilated bodies of 20 leading Bengali intellectuals were found on Dec. 18, and over 100 more in the next three days, subsequent investigation establishing that a massacre of intellectuals, technicians and professional men had taken place during the last stages of the war. Evidence of other massacres, involving many thousands of people, was discovered during the next few weeks.

Members of the Bangladesh Government finally arrived in the city on Dec. 22, the delay in their return being due to the Indian Army's wish to restore order before a civilian Government took over. The Cabinet was reshuffled and a list of measures drawn up to deal with immediate tasks.

Sheikh Mujibur Rahman, who had been arrested on the night of

March 25-26, 1971, and had been held ever since in West Pakistan, was released on Jan. 8, 1972, and flew to London, where he revealed that he had been sentenced to death in West Pakistan. On his return to Dacca on Jan. 10 he was given a tumultuous welcome, and two days later he resigned the presidency and became Prime Minister. Mr. Justice Abu Sayeed Chowdhury was sworn in as the new President of Bangladesh.

INTERNATIONAL SUPPORT FOR INDIA AND PAKISTAN

The United States had announced on Dec. 3, 1971, the cancellation of all outstanding licenses for shipment of military equipment to India, and all U.S. economic aid to India was suspended on Dec. 6. A State Department spokesman said that "the United States will not make a contribution to the Indian economy which will make it easier for the Indian Government to sustain its military effort", and that the question of similar action against Pakistan did not arise because all the aid in the pipeline was earmarked for humanitarian relief in East Pakistan.

President Nixon declared on Dec. 6 that he had "followed with sympathetic interest the efforts of the Government and people of Pakistan to achieve an amicable political settlement in East Pakistan", and that he welcomed "the efforts of President Yahya to move to reduce tensions on the subcontinent". In a television interview on the same day Mr. George Bush, the U.S. Ambassador to the United Nations, openly accused India of "clearcut aggression".

It was stated on Dec. 4 that India had invoked Article 9 of the Indo-Soviet Treaty of Peace, Friendship and Co-operation, which had been signed on Aug. 9, 1971, for an initial period of 20 years and which provided for consultations in the event of an attack or threatened attack upon either party.

The Soviet Government attributed the responsibility for the war to Pakistan in a statement issued by the official Tass agency on Dec. 5, and warned other Governments to avoid becoming involved in the conflict.

Chinese official statements attributed the entire responsibility for the war to India, and accused the Soviet Union of encouraging Indian "aggression".

MOVES TOWARDS PEACE, 1972

The opening of peace negotiations between India and Pakistan was delayed for some months, partly because of difficulties arising from Pakistan's refusal to recognize Bangladesh, and partly because the leaders of both countries made a number of visits to foreign countries in the first half of 1972 to obtain support for their respective positions.

The last Indian troops in Bangladesh were withdrawn on March 12, 1972, after a ceremonial parade in Dacca, 13 days earlier than the final date for their withdrawal announced on Feb. 8. Although the bulk of the troops had been withdrawn several weeks before, a number had remained in order to assist in the restoration of road, rail, river and air communications.

Mrs. Gandhi visited Dacca on March 17–19 for talks with Sheikh Mujib, with whom she signed a Joint Declaration and a Treaty of Friendship and Co-operation between India and Bangladesh.

Talks were held at Murree, near Rawalpindi, on April 26–29, 1972, by special emissaries from India and Pakistan, and a joint statement issued on April 30 said that they had settled the modalities for a meeting between President Bhutto and Mrs. Gandhi towards the end of May or the beginning of June.

The Simla Summit Conference

This conference between President Bhutto and Mrs. Gandhi opened on June 28, 1972, in Simla, which had been selected in preference to New Delhi because of a heat-wave in the Indian capital. In the absence of agreement (the main stumbling-block being Kashmir) the talks, which had been due to end on July 1, were extended for another day. An agreement was finally arrived at late on July 2, and was signed shortly after midnight.

The agreement contained the main elements of earlier Indian drafts, but the wording was considerably modified to make it acceptable to Pakistan. In particular, the clause referring to the cease-fire line in Kashmir was rephrased to read: "The line of control resulting from the cease-fire of Dec. 17, 1971, shall be respected by both sides without prejudice to the recognized position of either side."

The main text of the agreement was as follows:

"(I) The Government of India and the Government of Pakistan are resolved that the two countries put an end to the conflict and confrontation that have hitherto marred their relations and work for the promotion of friendly and harmonious relations and the establishment of durable peace in the subcontinent, so that both countries may henceforth devote their resources and energies to the pressing task of advancing the welfare of their peoples.

"In order to achieve this objective, the Government of India and the Government of Pakistan have agreed as follows:

(1) That the principles and purposes of the Charter of the United Nations shall govern the relations between the two countries.

(2) That the two countries are resolved to settle their differences by peaceful means through bilateral negotiations or by any other peaceful means mutually agreed upon between them. Pending the final settlement of any of the problems between the two countries, neither side shall unilaterally alter the situation and both shall prevent the organization, assistance or encouragement of any acts detrimental to the maintenance of peaceful and harmonious relations.

(3) That the prerequisite for reconciliation, good neighbourliness and durable peace between them is a commitment by both countries to peaceful coexistence, respect for each other's territorial integrity and sovereignty, and non-interference in each other's internal affairs, on the basis of equality and mutual benefit.

(4) That the basic issues and causes of conflict which have bedevilled the relations between the two countries for the past 25 years shall be resolved by peaceful means.

(5) That they shall always respect each other's national unity, territorial integrity, political independence and sovereign equality.

(6) That, in accordance with the Charter of the United Nations, they will refrain from the threat or use of force against the territorial integrity or political independence of each other.

"(II) Both Governments will take all steps within their power to prevent hostile propaganda directed against each other. Both countries will encourage dissemination of such information as would promote the development of friendly relations between them.

"(III) In order progressively to restore and normalize relations between the two countries step by step, it was agreed that:

(1) Steps shall be taken to resume communications—postal, telegraphic, sea, land, including border posts, and air links including overflights.

(2) Appropriate steps shall be taken to promote travel facilities for the nationals of the other country.

(3) Trade and co-operation in economic and other agreed fields will be resumed as far as possible.

(4) Exchanges in the fields of science and culture will be promoted.

In this connection, delegations from the two countries will meet from time to time to work out the necessary details.

"(IV) In order to initiate the process of the establishment of durable peace, both Governments agreed that:

(1) Indian and Pakistani forces shall be withdrawn to their side of the international border.

(2) In Jammu and Kashmir the line of control resulting from the cease-fire of Dec. 17, 1971, shall be respected by both sides without prejudice to the recognized position of either side. Neither side shall seek to alter it unilaterally, irrespective of mutual differences and legal interpretations. Both sides further undertake to refrain from the threat or use of force in violation of this line.

(3) The withdrawals shall commence upon the entry into force of this agreement, and shall be completed within a period of 30 days thereafter.

"(V) This agreement will be subject to ratification by both countries in accordance with their respective constitutional procedures and will come into force with effect from the date on which the instruments of ratification are exchanged.

"(VI) Both Governments agree that their respective Heads will meet again at a mutually convenient time in the future and that, in the meantime, representatives of the two sides will meet to discuss further the modalities and arrangements for the establishment of durable peace and normalization of relations, including the questions of repatriation of prisoners of war and civilian internees, a final settlement of Jammu and Kashmir, and the resumption of diplomatic relations."

The effect of the clauses relating to the withdrawal of forces and the cease-fire line in Kashmir was that Indian troops would be withdrawn from 5,139 square miles of Pakistani territory in the Punjab and Sind occupied during the war, and Pakistani troops from 69 square miles of Indian territory in the Punjab and Rajasthan. In Kashmir India would retain 480 square miles of territory west and north of the former cease-fire in the Poonch, Tithwal and Kargil sectors, and Pakistan 52 square miles east of the line in the Chhamb sector.

Following ratification by Pakistan on July 15 and by India on Aug 1–3, the agreement came into effect on Aug. 4, 1972.

APPENDIX I

PAKISTAN'S ALLIANCES

Although the Government of Pakistan had joined a number of alliances in the earlier years of Pakistan's existence, and Pakistan had received considerable material aid, including military equipment, in particular from the United States, her allies did not come to her aid during her various armed conflicts with India.

SOUTH EAST ASIA TREATY ORGANIZATION (SEATO)

Pakistan had on Sept. 8, 1954, signed the South East Asia Collective Defence Treaty (together with Australia, Britain, France, New Zealand, the Philippines, Thailand and the United States). This treaty was accompanied by (*a*) a unilateral U.S. declaration in the form of an "understanding" that the pact was directed against Communist aggression; (*b*) a Protocol on Indo-China; and (*c*) the "Pacific Charter", a general statement of principles, signed by all eight contracting parties.

At the 10th meeting of the SEATO Council in May 1965, the Pakistan representative made reservations on the Organization's political decisions on Vietnam and Laos, and also on the Malaysian-Indonesian dispute. From the Council's 12th meeting in 1967 Pakistan was no longer fully represented at Council meetings, and during the debate on the Simla Agreement President Bhutto announced on Jan. 14, 1972, that Pakistan had finally withdrawn from SEATO.

CENTRAL TREATY ORGANIZATION (CENTO)

Pakistan joined the Baghdad Pact (of mutual co-operation), a defence alliance and an organization for regional co-operation in the economic, cultural and technical fields, on Sept. 23, 1955—the Pact's other members being Britain, Iraq, Turkey and (from Nov. 3, 1955) Iran, with the United States as an associate member. Following the withdrawal of Iraq on March 24, 1959, the alliance's name was changed on Aug. 21, 1959, to Central Treaty Organization (CENTO).

Bilateral treaties concluded by CENTO members included a defence agreement between the United States and Pakistan, signed on March 5, 1959, under which the U.S.A. undertook to supply Pakistan with "such military and economic assistance as may be mutually agreed upon". Such assistance was to be used by Pakistan for its security and defence in conformity with an earlier Joint Declaration issued by the Ministerial Council of the Baghdad Pact on July 28, 1958.

REGIONAL CO-OPERATION FOR DEVELOPMENT (RCD)

A group known as Regional Co-operation for Development (RCD) "parallel to but outside CENTO" was established by the Heads of State of Iran, Pakistan and Turkey on July 20–21, 1964. The Organization has, through its Ministerial Council assisted by a Regional Planning Council and numerous subcommittees, set up a considerable number of schemes for co-operation between the three countries, among them a Regional Cultural Institute, a tripartite Shipping Conference and a joint Chamber of Commerce and Industry.

A bilateral agreement on friendly co-operation between Turkey and Pakistan, signed on April 2, 1954, provided *inter alia* for consultation and co-operation in the field of defence.

OTHER TREATIES

Other treaties concluded by Pakistan included:
(*a*) a Treaty of Perpetual Peace and Friendship with Burma, signed on June 25, 1952;
(*b*) an agreement on economic and technical co-operation with China, details of which were not disclosed, signed in Peking during a visit by President Yahya Khan on Nov. 10–14, 1970. In a joint com-

muniqué signed at the end of this visit, China reaffirmed its "firm support to the people of Pakistan in their struggle for the defence of national independence".

On April 12, 1971, the Chinese Foreign Minister sent to President Yahya Khan a message expressing China's "full support", in particular if "Indian expansionists" should "dare to launch aggression against Pakistan".

During a visit to Peking by a Pakistani delegation led by Mr. Bhutto on Nov. 5–8, 1971, the Chinese acting Foreign Minister assured his visitors that "should Pakistan be subjected to foreign aggression the Chinese Government and people will, as always, resolutely support the Pakistan Government in their struggle to defend their State sovereignty and national independence". China's support for Pakistan was strongly reaffirmed by other Chinese leaders later in November 1971.

APPENDIX II

HEADS OF GOVERNMENT AND OF STATE, 1947–1971

Prime Ministers

LIAQUAT ALI KHAN. Aug. 15, 1947 (assassinated October 1951)
KHWAJA NAZIMUDDIN. Oct. 17, 1951 (Government dismissed April 1953)
MOHAMMED ALI. April 17, 1953 (resigned August 1955)
CHAUDHRI MOHAMMAD ALI. Aug. 12, 1955 (resigned August 1956)
HUSSEIN SHAHEED SUHRAWARDY. Sept. 12, 1956 (resigned October 1957)
ISMAIL IBRAHIM CHUNDRIGAR. Oct. 19, 1957 (resigned December 1957)
FIROZ KHAN NOON. Dec. 16, 1957 (dismissed October 1958)
Martial law imposed under GENERAL MOHAMMED AYUB KHAN on Oct. 7, 1958.

Presidents

ISKANDER MIRZA. March 23, 1956
MOHAMMED AYUB KHAN. Oct. 28, 1958
YAHYA KHAN. March 31, 1969
ZULFIQAR ALI BHUTTO. Dec. 20, 1971

RECOMMENDED FURTHER READING

ALI, Chaudhri Mohammad, *Emergence of Pakistan*. (Columbia University Press, 1967.)

AZIZ, Khursheed Kamal, *The Making of Pakistan: A Study in Nationalism*. (Chatto & Windus, 1967.)

BURKE, S. M., *Pakistan's Foreign Policy*. (Oxford University Press, 1972.)

CALLARD, Keith, *Pakistan: A Political Study*. (Allen & Unwin, 1957.)

CHAUDHURI, G. W., *Constitutional Development in Pakistan*. (Longman, 1970.)

FALCON, Walter P., and PAPANEK, Gustav F. (ed.), *Development Policy. Vol. 2: The Pakistan Experience*. (Harvard University Press, 1972.)

FELDMAN, Herbert, *From Crisis to Crisis*. (Oxford University Press, 1972.)

FELDMAN, Herbert, *Revolution in Pakistan*. (Oxford University Press, 1967.)

GLEDHILL, Alan, *Pakistan*. (Stevens & Sons, 1964.)

GOSWAMI, B. N., *Pakistan and China: A Study of their Relations*. (Allied Publishers, Bombay, 1972.)

HUSSAIN, Arih, *Pakistan: Its Ideology and Foreign Policy*. (Frank Cass, 1966.)

India's Relations with Pakistan, (Asia Publishing House, Bombay, 1968.)

JHA, Dinesh Chandra, *Indo-Pakistan Relations (1960–1965)*. (Patna: Bharati Bhawan, 1972.)

McDONOUGH, Sheila (ed.), *Mohammed Ali Jinnah, Maker of Modern Pakistan*. (D. C. Heath, 1971.)

PAPANEK, Gustav F., *Pakistan's Development*. (Harvard University Press, 1968.)

SAYEED, Khalid B., *Pakistan: The Formative Phase, 1857–1945*. (Oxford University Press, 1968.)

SINGH, Sangat, *Pakistan's Foreign Policy*. (Asia Publishing House, Bombay, 1970.)

VORYS, Karl von, *Political Development in Pakistan*. (Princeton University Press, 1966.)

WEEKES, R. V. *Pakistan: Birth and Growth of a Muslim Nation*. (Van Nostrand Reinhold, 1965.)

WHEELER, Richard S., *Politics of Pakistan: A Constitutional Quest*. (Cornell University Press, 1970.)

WILCOX, Wayne Ayres, *Pakistan: The Consolidation of a Nation*. (Columbia University Press, 1964.)

WILLIAMS, L. F. Rushbrook, *State of Pakistan*. (Faber and Faber, 1966.)

INDEX

INDEX

A
Ahmadiya sect, 26
Ali, Hamid, 70
Ali, Mohammed, *see* Mohammed Ali
Ali, Shahed, 71
All-Moslem Parties' Convention, 26
Amin, Nurul, 100
Amjad Ali, Syed, 71, 72
Assam, 7, 87
Attlee, Clement, 3, 7, 45
Aurora, General Jagjit Singh, 121
Awami League, 61, 64, 66–72, 81, 85, 95–8, 100, 108–9, 111
    General elections, 105–7
Awami Moslem League, 31, 35
Ayub Khan, Mohammed, 30, 56, 72–3, 76–85, 86, 88, 94–103, 131
Azad Pakistan Party, 30, 61

B
Bahawalpur, 6, 23, 64–5, 103
Baluchistan
    (*see also* Kalat, 4–6, 14, 23, 64, 66, 103, 107
Bangladesh, 111, 113–16, 118–24, 125
    (For events prior to proclamation of Republic of Bangladesh *see under* East Pakistan, subheading Civil War)
    Independence, 111, 113
    India, Treaty of Friendship and Co-operation, 125
Bashani, Maulana, 69
Basic Democracies, 76–8, 97–9
Bengal
    (*see also* East Bengal and East Pakistan), 7–8, 9
Bhutto, Zulfiqar Ali, 51, 91, 94–5, 98, 104–6, 107–10, 123, 125, 131
Bills
    Acquired Territories Merger Bill, 1961, 44

137

Constitution Bill, 1956, 61
Constitution (Second Amendment) Bill, 1964, 82
Constitution (Ninth Amendment) Bill, 1961, 44
Elections Bill, 1964, 83
Electoral College Bill, 1964, 82
Electoral Rolls Bill, 1957, 67
Electorate Amendment Bill, 1957, 67
Electorate Bill, 1956, 67
Establishment of West Pakistan Bill, 1955, 64, 67
Fundamental Rights Bill, 1963, 82
Indian Independence Bill, 1947, 3
Political Parties Bill, 1962, 80
Presidential Election Bill, 1964, 83
Preventive Detention Laws Amendment Bill, 1962, 81
Representation of the People Bill, 1957, 67
Border Incidents (1956), 42; (1958–59), 43–4; (1965), 88–9
  Rann of Kutch, 88–9
  Kashmir, *see* separate heading
Boundaries
  Acquired Territories Merger Bill (1961), 44
  Bagge Tribunal, 41–2
  Bengal, 9
  Constitution (Ninth Amendment) Bill (1961), 44
  Discussions (1953), 42; (1958), 43–4; (1959), 86; (1960), 86
  Punjab, 10
  Radcliffe Commission, 9–10
  Rann of Kutch, 89
British plan for partition (June 1947), 3, 6, 7
Burma, 129

C
Canal Waters, 52–8
  Indus Waters Treaty, 56–7
Capital, 5, 14–15
Central Treaty Organization (CENTO), 69, 129
China, 47, 123–4, 129–30
Choudhury, Hamidul Huq, 71
Chowdhury, Abu Sayeed, 124
Chundrigar, Ismail Ibrahim, 131
Communal Disorders (1946–47), 10–11, 13; (1950), 39; (1954), 34; (1961), 87; (1962), 87; (1963), 51; (1964), 87–8
  Anti-Ahmadiya demonstrations, 26
  Delhi Conference, 1964, 88
Constituent Assembly, 4–5, 14, 27–30, 32–3, 59–61, 66
  "Punjab group", 27, 29
  "East Bengal group", 27, 29
  Moslem League Assembly Party, 27, 29, 36, 68
  Constituent Convention, 60
  Emergency Powers Ordinance, 60
Constitution, 1956, 60–4, 66, 69, 72, 82
  Abrogation, 72, 78
  Basic Principles Committee, 17–21, 23–4, 29
  Constituent Convention, 60
  Constitution Amendment Act (1954), 24–5

138

Directive Principles of State Policy, 21
Fundamental Rights Committee, 22
Objectives Resolution (1949), 18, 21, 24
Preparatory work, 17–24, 29
(*see also* Bills)
Constitution, 1962, 66, 76, 79–80, 99
Constitution Commission, 77, 79
Provisional Constitution Order, 1969, 99
Constitutional Developments, 100–3
Abrogation, 99
(*see also* Bills)
Cooch-Behar, 40, 44
Cripps Mission, 1942, 2

D
Daultana, Mian Mumtaz, 26–7, 30
Democratic Action Committee, 97–8
Democratic Group, 81

E
East Bengal
(*see also* East Pakistan and Bengal), 5, 8, 14, 64
East Pakistan
(*see also* East Bengal and Bengal)
Area and population, 5, 9, 32, 65, 96, 107
Assembly prorogued (1956), 69; (1958), 70; reconvened, 70; dissolved, 71
Autonomist movement, 95–100

Bangladesh, *see* separate heading
Civil war, 107–13
Communal disorders (1954), 34; (1961), 87; (1962), 87; (1964), 87
Constitution suspended, 68–9
East Pakistan National Democratic Front, 95
East Punjab (India)
Renamed Punjab, 10
Elections
Basic Democracy units, 77
Electoral college, 83
General, 104–7
National Assembly, 85
Presidential, 84
Provincial Assembly, 85, 107
(*see also* Bills)
Electorates, separate and joint, 66–7

F
Farman Ali Khan, General, 121
Firoz Khan Noon, *see* Noon, Firoz Khan
Food crisis (1953), 25; (1955–56), 68
Frontier States (Chitral, Dir, Swat), 4, 6–7, 23, 64

G
Gandhi, Indira, 115–17, 121, 125
Gandhi, Mohandas Kamamchand (Mahatma), 10, 16
Ghaffar Khan, Khan Abdul, 13–14
Ghulam Mohammed, 27, 29–30, 34, 60
Government of India Act, 1935, 24, 26; amendment, 28–9
Graham, Frank P., 51

H
Hakim, Abdul, 70, 71
Huq, Fazlul, 32, 34–5, 68–70

I
Iftikhar Hussain, Khan of Mamdot, 36
India, relations with
    Bangladesh, recognition, 119, refugees, 113–16
    Indo-Pakistan war, *see* separate heading
    Kashmir, *see* separate heading
    Nehru-Mohammed Ali talks (1954), 40
    Rann of Kutch hostilities (1965), 88–9
Indian Independence Act, 3–4, 26
Indo-Pakistan war (1971), 118–23
    Attacks on Pakistani forces, 117
    Civil war, tension following, 115–16
    Fighting on East Pakistan border, 117
    Gandhi, Mrs., visits abroad, 116
    International support, 124
    Jessore offensive, 117–18
    Map, 122
    Refugees, 113–16
    Security Council Resolution, 122–3
    Simla agreement, 125–7; ratification, 127
    State of Emergency, 118
    Surrender, 120–1
    U.N. offer of good offices, 117
International Bank for Reconstruction and Development, 54–6
Ipi, Fakir of, 14

Islamic Republic of Pakistan, 17, 24, 62, 64, 82, 102

J
Jacob, Major-General J. F. R., 120
Jamaat-i-Islami, 30, 81, 85, 95, 105
Jarring, Gunnar, 51
Jinnah-Awami League, 30–1
Jinnah, Fatima, 83–5
Jinnah, Mohammed Ali, 1–3, 6, 10, 14–16, 32
Junagadh, 8–9
Justice Party, 100

K
Kalat (*see also* Baluchistan), 5–6, 65
Kashmir
    Accession to India, 45
    "*Azad* Kashmir", 46–7, 90
    Border incidents (1947), 45
    Canal waters, 52
    Cease-fire (1948), 47; (1965), 91
    China-Pakistan agreement, 47
    Constitution, 49–50
    Crisis of 1965, 90–1
    Five-point peace plan, 49
    Graham report, 51
    Jarring mission, 51
    Kashmir Commission, 46–7
    Security Council, resolutions, 46, 90–1; meeting (1957), 50–1
    Tashkent Declaration, 91–3
    Theft of relic (1963), 51
    Truce line, 49; troop concentrations (1966), 93; New Delhi talks, 93; violations after civil war, 117
    (*see also* Maps)

Kathiawar States, 8–9
Khairpur, 4, 23, 64–5
Khan Sahib, Dr., 28, 30, 68
Khilafat-e-Rabani, 31
Khuhro, M. A., 35–6
Kosygin, Alexei, 91
Krishak Sramik, 31–2, 35, 70–1, 81

L

Language, 19–20, 32–3, 64, 79
Legal Framework Order, 1970, 101–3
Liaquat Ali Khan, 2, 18–19, 32, 39–40, 49, 131
Lucknow Pact, 15

M

Malik, A. M., 119, 121
Mandal, Jogendra Nath, 40
Manekshaw, General Sam, 119–21
Maps
    Canal waters, 53
    East Pakistan, 112; Indian-occupied towns at time of surrender, 122
    Kashmir cease-fire line, 48
    Pakistan, 74–5
Martial law, 72, 78, 80, 94, 99, 104, 109
Minorities
    Calcutta Agreement (1948), 37–8
    Hindus, 40–1
    Karachi talks (1950), 39
    New Delhi Agreement (1948), 38; (1950), 39, 49
Mirza, Iskander, 30, 34, 64–5, 68–9, 72–3, 131

Mohammad Ali, Chaudhri, 42, 68–9, 100, 131
Mohammed Ali, 26–30, 32, 35, 40, 47, 56, 61, 64, 131
Moslem League, 2–3, 5, 15–16, 19, 27, 29, 30–2, 36, 64, 66, 105, 108
    "Conventionists", 81, 83, 85, 105
    "Council group", 81, 85, 90, 95, 105
    "Non-revivalists", 81
    Pakistan resolution, 2, 85
    Revival (1962), 81
Moslem State of Pakistan, 2, 85
Moslems, percentages, 4–5, 9–10
Mountbatten, Lord, 1, 3
Mudie, Sir Francis, 36
Mujibur Rahman, Sheikh, 35, 81, 96–7, 104, 106–13, 123–5
Mukti Bahini, 115, 117–20, 123
Mukti Fouj, see Mukti Bahini

N

National Assembly, 62, 66, 71, 81–3, 101–2, 107–10
National Awami Party, 68–70, 81, 85, 95, 97, 105, 107, 115
National Democratic Front, 81, 95, 100
Nazimuddin, Khwaja, 16, 20–1, 25–7, 29, 131
Nehru, Jawaharlal, 16, 39–43, 45–7, 49, 54–6, 86, 88
Niazi, Amin Abdullah Khan, 120–1
Nixon, Richard M., 124
Nizam-i-Islam, 31, 35, 66, 81, 85, 95, 100
Noon, Firoz Khan, 27, 43, 50–1, 71–2, 86, 131

141

"Noon group", 61
North-West Frontier Province, 4, 6, 13–14, 23, 30–1, 33, 64–5, 103, 107
  Pathanistan, 13–14

P

Pakistan Democratic Movement, 95, 97
Pakistan Democratic Party, 100, 105
Pakistan National Congress, 61, 64
Pakistan People's Party (N.-W. Frontier Province), 14
Pakistan People's Party (West Pakistan), 95, 104–5, 106–8
Pathanistan, 13–14
People's Councils, 98
People's Democratic Group, 81
Political parties (*see also* separate headings)
  Suppression, 72
  Political activity resumed, 101; banned, 111; Regulation, 100–1
  Political Parties Bill (1962), 80–1
  Revival, 80–1
Population
  West Pakistan, 4–5, 65
  East Pakistan, 5, 9, 32, 65, 96, 107
PRODA (Public and Representative Offices [Disqualification] Act), 29, 36
Provinces (*see also* separate provinces), 63, 64–6, 72, 79
  Developments (1951–54), 30–6
  "Provincial list", 28
  Relationship with Central Government, 19, 27–30, 102
  Representation in Central Legislature, 27–8
Provincial Reorganization Committee, 78
Provisional Constitution Order, 99
Punjab, 4, 7, 10–14, 23, 27, 29, 30–1, 36, 64–5, 103, 106–7
  Canal waters, 52–8
  Name changed, 10

Q

Quaid-i-Azam, see Jinnah, Mohammed Ali

R

Rahman, Sheikh Mujibur, *see* Mujibur Rahman, Sheikh
Rahman Khan, Ataur, 69–70, 81
Rann of Kutch, 88–9
Rashid Khan, Abdur, 68
Razakars, 115–16, 119, 123
Redshirt Organization, 13, 31
Refugees, 10–13, 37–41, 87, 113–16
Regional Co-operation for Development (RCD), 129
Republican Party, 66–8, 81

S

Sarkar, Abu Hussain, 69–71
Sattar, Pirzada Abdus, 28, 36, 65, 100
Scheduled Castes Federation, 61
Shastri, Lal Bahadur, 88, 93
Simla agreement, 125–7
Sind, 4–5, 14–15, 23, 27, 30, 35–6, 64–5, 103, 106–7
South East Asia Treaty Organization (SEATO), 69, 128

Soviet Union, 91, 116–17, 123–4
State of Emergency, 27, 30, 90, 97–8, 118
Statement of June 3, 1947, 3, 6–7
Student unrest, 94–5, 98–9
Suhrawardy, Hussein Shaheed, 8, 69, 71
Sylhet, 7, 14

T

Tashkent Declaration (1966), 91–2
Thant, U, 117
Treaty of Friendship and Co-operation (India-Bangladesh), 125
Treaty of Peace, Friendship and Co-operation (India-Soviet Union), 124
Treaty of Perpetual Peace and Friendship (Burma-Pakistan), 129
Turkey
  Agreement on friendly co-operation, 129

U

United Front (*Juqta*), 31, 34, 61, 64, 66–7, 69

United Progressive Parliamentary Party, 61, 64
United States, 25, 46, 124, 128–9

W

Waziristan, 14
West Pakistan (*see also* separate provinces)
  Administrative changes, 78
  Area and population, 4–5, 65
  Constitution, 68
  Establishment of West Pakistan Bill (1955), 64, 67–8
  Federal Legislature, representation, 17–20, 23, 27
  One-unit system, 27–8, 64–6, 67; reversion to provinces proposed, 68, 100–1
  Political developments (1956–57), 67–8
  Student unrest, 94–5, 98
West Punjab, *see* Punjab
World Bank, 54–6

Y

Yahya Khan, Mohammed, 93–4, 99, 111, 115, 117–19, 121–2, 129–31
  Resignation, 123